Your Way

Starting Your Own SMALL BUSINESS in RURAL SOUTH DAKOTA on Farms, Ranches and in Small Towns

by
Tom Kilian

Library of Congress
Catalog Card No. 97-93128

ISBN 1-57579-062-9

Printed in United States of America

PINE HILL PRESS, INC.
Freeman, S. Dak. 57029

CONTENTS

FOREWORD

Someone has said, "Home is where the heart is." For most people, home is the place of their earliest memories: the house where they grew up; the yards and fields in which they played as kids, the schoolhouse, the family friends and neighbors and the things that these people believed and did during their early years.

South Dakota is one of our country's most rural states—lots of open country between Buffalo and Elk Point, lots of room between farms and ranches, lots of space and lots of sky. South Dakotans learn to watch the clouds and sky, to see what's coming, weatherwise. It gets to be second nature.

There are so many things that blend together to make rural South Dakota: the smell of a fresh-cut stubble field at sundown. The entire air full of the smell of blooming yellow clover. The smell of a dry summer pasture full of rosen weed. The summer picnics and the family reunions, church socials, set out in the shade of the cottonwood grove.

The bright lilt of the Meadowlark from a weathered fence post may be about the closest thing there is to capturing South Dakota. And, all the sounds of all the winds: the howls of winter, the roar of a summer afternoon storm, cut by the electric cracks of lightning and earth-shaking booms of thunder. The fresh lift of seeing and smelling a patch of wild roses in a grassy ditch. The black silhouettes of hilltops against a blaze-of-orange sunset. The muted cackles and chirps of redwing blackbirds across a cattail slough. The weathered faces of people old when we were young. There is no end of sounds and smells and shadings of light and color, and the shapes of buildings and the lay of the landscape, woven together that speak to us of home. The night sky almost white with stars in so huge a space that it helps us to understand a little better who we are.

The things in rural South Dakota that catch and hold us are things that money can't buy. Quiet rural places shape our thinking and our lives. Our surroundings help to educate us wherever we are. It is not really possible to grow up in really rural South Dakota and not be molded by the experiences.

One often hears the expression: South Dakota is a great place to raise a family. Young couples say "We came back from wherever so we could raise our kids in a place like this." South Dakota is a great place for kids and for the kids that never grow up inside, the adults who live here, too.

While it is sometimes hard to put into words, there are reasons why most of the people who live on farms, ranches and small towns all across South Dakota want to stay. These reasons are why many of them never left. Even when making enough money to pay the bills is hard, many people want to stay and live in this place. That is what this book is about: helping people who want to stay in rural South Dakota to start their own business and earn their own living, so they can live in a place that means "home" to them.

THE PRAIRIE TOWN TOMORROW

As South Dakota's population silently shifts from country to town, some people worry if there will be anyone left in the rural areas in the time to come. There are endless meetings in small town halls and cafes about what can be done to create new jobs so people can live there. Some people want to bring back the retail stores so it will be a "full-service community" again, as it was a generation ago.

Invention and technology have changed things greatly. New machines that do almost everything faster and easier have changed our ways of life. More work is done by fewer people. We travel and communicate faster, farther. Many of the towns of our parents' day are simply not needed anymore. Such towns cannot be restored to be as they were. The need for them is simply gone. We can no more stop technological change than we can stop the wind.

OLD TOWNS—NEW JOBS

Many of our small towns can survive change and become places where people doing new things can call them home. In the future, the people who live in our small towns will be making their living in new ways. They may run a crafts shop or a meat locker or a welding shop or grow organic foods. There will be a convenience store where they can get gas, milk, eggs, and junk food. Some towns will have small plants processing ag products or producing a great variety of consumer goods. Very slowly, more people will move in from distant urban areas, tired of the battle there.

WHERE NEW LITTLE BUSINESSES COME FROM

Most new little businesses are started and operated by individuals and families—not by economic development committees and boards. The tiny, new businesses that can stabilize and build South Dakota's rural towns are far too small to interest most economic developers. Most small business start-ups are by individuals who believe their ideas will work. They do the footwork, sign for the start-up loans and work night and day to make them go. Development committees can encourage, but they don't *do*.

Those small towns that survive will become the locations of new tiny businesses and the homes of those who start them. It is sensible to do all we can to encourage such people and help them make it. They are the only ones who can "save" the small towns: the people who work and live in them. So, let's find and help these people.

CHAPTER I

THE PURPOSE OF THIS BOOK

The central purpose of this book is to help people who live on farms, ranches, or in small towns to start and operate small businesses, to increase family income and enable them to continue to live where they are.

CENTRAL MESSAGE OF THIS BOOK

Hopefully, this book will help you to look at earning an income in ways different from what you have been doing up to now—or perhaps even thought about seriously. When most people think about earning a living, they assume one thing: they have got to find a job, working for someone else who is willing to hire them.

This book can help you to look at job hunting differently. The secret: you don't have to hunt for a job: you can invent or create your own.

THE ONE-WAY TICKET

We are not taught to think this way in modern society. For most everyone, school means the way we prepare ourselves to get a job—to work for someone else. We go to high school, get a diploma or a GED certificate to encourage someone to hire us. We go to college or a technical institute so that we will have a better chance of getting hired—by someone else. We are taught how to compose a slick resume which tries to make us appear as attractive as possible to someone we hope will give us a job.

Hardly anyone even thinks of creating his own job, to work for himself. We can go from preschool through the university and never once be faced with the idea that maybe we should cook up something to do ourselves rather than to plan our whole lives on the idea of working for someone else.

Farmers and ranchers work for themselves, but the majority of farm and ranch families are taking jobs off the place to get enough cash income to be able to stay there. Wouldn't it be better to create and operate the other job yourself? If there are profits, you get to keep them.

In many rural settings these days, jobs are scarce; pay is low and will barely reach around. So, some folks run—literally—between two or even three jobs, trying to hang on. In really rural spots, very few jobs exist. If you live in such a place you may have to create your own job if you are going to live there.

IDEAS FROM THE PAST

In the past, many South Dakotans have believed:

1) There are only a couple of ways to make a living in rural areas. If you farm, you must be or try to become a part of big ag—a part of production agriculture. You must use big machines, big loads of chemicals, seeds from mainline suppliers, deal with big processors—all encouraged and egged on by the big agribusiness corporations, the federal Department of Agriculture and the state agricultural colleges.

2) If you don't farm, only a few kinds of businesses are possible in a rural area: the small retail and service businesses on

main street—grocery, hardware, barber shop, gas, and repairs. They are the only ones visible, close-up.

3) So it follows: if one doesn't farm or run a retail store, the only other possibility is to work for someone else (get a job in the courthouse, school, cafe, bank, or prepare to be a teacher, nurse, or mechanic).

HOW DID WE GET THIS WAY?

In the past, and too often today, our school system has failed utterly to teach students that they need not necessarily work for someone else when they finish school. They were never told that they might plan, start, and run their own business. The present educational system has evolved essentially to serve business and the corporation—with considerable encouragement from them to do so. It was designed to supply people trained to fit the schedule, behavior, and skill needs of the office and factory. As high school and college students approach graduation, they are urged to prepare for the "job interview." They are told to expect to be screened for work—for someone else. It never seems to have occurred to many educators and school boards that courses pointed toward running one's *own* business are a possible option.

KEEP OUR KIDS AT HOME

Candidates for political office and professional community boosters are fond of announcing plans to attract "jobs" that will keep young people from moving off to the city. The implicit assumption is that if one works at all, it is for somebody else. Community developers might be equally well employed in trying to identify the people in their home counties who have ideas, to help them start and operate their own businesses—and to help young people learn that they can, too.

CHANGE COMES SLOWLY

In very recent years, schools have made some beginnings in encouraging students to start their own businesses. A noble effort has been launched at Agar, South Dakota, by Dr. George Levin, to operate a high school devoted to entrepreneurial studies. There are lip-service efforts in high schools across the state in the form of business shadowing programs, lectures by business leaders in the school, field trips and the like. Most business and trade associations push for "cooperative" programs with the schools, most of which are really efforts to improve the student's image and perception of the business community. Most of this effort never really makes the point at all: business is presented as a place where one can get a job, not a process in which the student can start and run his own enterprise.

CHANGES IN THE WORKPLACE

In recent years, employment practices have changed dramatically. Because of automation, huge corporate lay-offs, the exporting of jobs overseas, and a blizzard of electronic devices for communication and data processing, industrial jobs are disappearing rapidly. Good paying jobs today are increasingly in the professions and science-related technology. Most jobs available now are in low-paying service fields, in food service, cleaning, repairs, custodial and the like. And most such jobs are fairly limited in rural areas such as South Dakota. Far fewer of them are needed.

If there is anything to be learned from these changes, it is that there may be real merit in creating your own business, in your own community, doing something you would like to do and building a secure future, right where you are.

IT'S NOT FOR EVERYONE

Not everyone who thinks of starting a new business can or will. Basic to the process is that one must really *want* to do it. One must want to do it for reasons other than simply making money. If making money is one's only goal and he doesn't care much how he does it, it will be harder to choose a business and still harder to succeed in it. Of course, money is important. Of course, we all want to have a comfortable income. But it is terribly important to do something we enjoy, want to do, and, if possible, love to do. Money is more likely to be a by-product of that.

PEOPLE VARY

Early on, it must be made plain: running one's own business is not for everyone. Some people:

—are not suited for it—it's hard for them to make decisions.
—lack confidence in their own ideas.
—lack the patience to hang on and keep going.
—don't want to or can't handle the responsibility.
—have limiting health problems or family obligations.
—lack the judgement and common sense to make the right moves.
—don't have the energy, determination, or drive to succeed.
—just plain don't want to, for whatever reasons.

Dorothy R. in Moody county began making home-made soap from a recipe she got from her grandmother. It was really good soap; it looked good, smelled good, and worked good. People liked it and wanted more. Elmer J. in Hyde County designed and built a solid and really attractive three-legged stool for his granddaughter. People saw it and wanted one, too.

He began building more stools. But Dorothy and Elmer both decided they didn't want to have the pressures of time and energy that larger production would require. Demand for their products was clear. They could build and grow and make some money. But they decided building a small business wasn't for them.

We are not all alike and we don't have the same interests and goals. Thank heaven, we don't. If everyone wanted to start his own business, there wouldn't be anyone left to work in them all. But not to worry. We are in no imminent danger of having too many folks trying to do so.

This book may help some people who might be better off if they don't try to start and run their own business. It might save a lot of disappointment, heartbreak and lost savings in the process.

THE BOTTOM LINE

If you are going to create your own business, you must plan to offer something that people: 1) want 2) can't or won't do for themselves, and 3) are willing to pay you for.

Whatever you do, it will likely be an improvement or change on a product or service that already exists. If it's a food, maybe you change its shape, appearance, color, flavor, texture, or nutritional value. Your version must be seen as attractive for some reason—and it may be only in a clever new name or a more appealing package.

You may say "I'd like to do such and such, but there is already a guy in Watertown who's doing the same thing." That's where we get down to business. First, try to find out what is really happening in Watertown. Maybe it's all talk, with nothing much happening. Maybe mistakes are being made in the quality or usefulness or appearance of the Watertown product. Don't assume that everyone is going to build a successful business just because they've started. Maybe what you learn will cause you to re-think your plan, but don't assume you are defeated before you're sure.

Many people mistakenly feel that because there are already dozens, hundreds, of types and flavors of cookies on the market, there's no room for a new cookie. Wrong, very wrong. There is always room for variety and improvements. A competitive market is based on the idea that someone or something is going to come along to replace the old champion. It was ever thus, since humans started making stone tools.

So, you might be thinking of food, clothing, gift items, a day-care, tools, furniture garden equipment, an office service, or any of thousands of different products. There are endless things that could be manufactured or produced in South Dakota, but which are not simply because no one has gone ahead and done it.

THE MOTHER OF INVENTION

If you need income and live on a farm near White Lake, a ranch near Leola, or in a small town like Viborg or Castlewood, and you want to continue to live where you are, you have to choose a business that can succeed in your location. If your home's location is important to you, this will give you the motivation to work hard to figure out how to succeed. Sure, you could maybe do it somewhere else—maybe even more easily—but you don't want to be somewhere else! That is the critical fact. So, your business will have to work where you are. Necessity really can be the mother of invention. If we feel we must, it is often surprising what we can do. We simply figure out how, if it is important enough. The desire to live in a particular location can be a very powerful influence on our choices of work. It affects the choices of millions of people every year—people moving from city to suburb and from suburb to the countryside, and vice versa.

BUILDING A SERVICE BUSINESS

In some really rural areas, like Billsburo or Millboro, there simply may not be enough people who need a specific kind of service to make it go. If there aren't enough kids close by, a day-care isn't going to work. But it is also true that new communications and shipping systems make many services possible that were not a few years ago. For some kinds of businesses, it is getting less and less important where you live. The quality, value, and cost of your product has always mattered, but it looms much larger now.

PRODUCING PRODUCTS ANYWHERE—ALMOST

In earlier times, many people felt that it was not possible to manufacture most products for market in South Dakota. There were too few people close by to buy stuff and freight charges were too high to reach more populous markets. So almost all business activity was geared toward farming and extraction of natural resources. For small manufactured items it is far less true today with vast improvements in delivery services, both air and ground. Today it is possible to manufacture many products almost anywhere and ship them to areas where there are more buyers.

CHAPTER II

CHOOSING THE RIGHT BUSINESS

DO SOMETHING YOU ENJOY

Almost everyone will agree that we do better when we work at something we enjoy. The reasons are simple: if we are interested we will want to learn how to do it better and we will remember what we learn. We try harder because we want good results. We are more highly motivated. We get a sense of satisfaction in doing something well that we care about. And, we are often more successful because buyers are attracted to people who enjoy their work. Enjoyment simply shows; one can sense it.

Fine, you say, but who gets to do that? I can't make any money doing anything I like! Are you sure? For starters, try making a list of things you do enjoy: cooking? fishing? woodworking? dancing? sewing? gardening? collecting guns?

Most of us spend from 40 to 50 years of our lives working. It makes sense that we try to work at something we enjoy, since we won't be coming by a second time. Probably, no one plans to have an unhappy work life. It happens from just drifting along, pillar to post, and not really planning to make sure it doesn't happen. There is lots we can do about our future if we just try.

DO SOMETHING OTHERS WILL ENJOY

There are hundreds of ways of creating a business of the most ordinary, common pastimes. People usually manage to find money enough to buy the things they really want. George J. just bought a new shotgun. Did he need it? No. Did he want it? Yes. He bought it at a farm-based gun shop in Codington County.

There is no food so common that new or improved variations cannot attract new buyers. If you like gardening or growing things, raising rare, unusual or decorative plants can attract buyers who can't find them in conventional greenhouses or the mall discount stores.

In an increasingly complicated, automated, chip-directed world, almost anything *handmade* will attract people who are bone-tired of mass-produced, impersonally produced, cookie-cutter products. They want to feel that a human hand has touched it, cared about it. If you care about the products you produce, it will show. People will see the originality in it. Your personal touch will shine through and touch them.

NEW WINE IN OLD SKINS

James Burke, the British writer, has produced some fascinating books in which he shows us how inventions evolve and get improved upon over time. Most of the products we use every day are not brand-new ideas. They are simply improved, simplified, re-designed versions of older, earlier ideas. The dried strips of buffalo meat that traditional Sioux Indians made are called "Jerky" in flashy plastic packages in gas stations and hiker's backpacks everywhere. Scarves have evolved into ski masks. Grandpa's crank telephone is now cellular. Grandma's big chunks of baking chocolate are now trim little chips in plastic bags.

SEEING WITH NEW EYES

Albert Einstein once said, "Imagination is more powerful than knowledge." Part of the secret of finding/inventing new products comes from *looking at common ordinary things around us with a new eye.* It can be interesting and a lot of fun. Since you live in a rural area, consider an item that is everywhere: an old, weathered cedar fence post. If you were going to make something different out of it—recycle it—what could it become? You could shape it into book ends, a lamp stand, a floral centerpiece, a boot stand, a coat rack, a frame for a painting, and on and on. Suppose you made something like that—could you sell it? What if you had access to lots of old cedar posts?

Around farms and small towns there are enormous resources of this kind: piles of old rusty iron and junk; tangles of old barbed wire; old, weathered, gray farm buildings; wetlands full of unusual plants; long reaches of natural prairie full of wild flowers, grasses and dozens of other plants; piles of stones in fence corners; old farm groves and wind breaks, old windmills and so on. All of this is waiting for someone with imagination to convert them into something else. These resources are from low to no cost. They can be converted into hundreds of different products. Without being tedious, you get the picture. Look at the old, ordinary, and commonplace with a new eye. Use your imagination. Ask yourself what it could become.

REUSING THE PAST

There are over 400 small towns in South Dakota, stretching from White Rock to Ardmore. Most of them have empty store fronts, abandoned brick bank buildings, lodge halls, churches, and hundreds of old weathered farmsteads scattered everywhere.

Every one of these old places is a monument to a way of life that was yesterday. The society that built these buildings has gone the way of the passenger pigeon. To the people who were born in or who were young in such places, it may be a sad sight. But for today, this array of artifacts of the past is an enormous treasure, full of opportunities!

Who would be interested in these weathered relics? Who could see opportunity in this panorama of ruin? Well, among others:

—Antique collectors and dealers
—Metal sculptors
—Restoration builders and designers
—Decorators, interior and exterior
—Picture framers
—Welding shops and blacksmiths
—Museums, galleries
—Small manufacturers
—Wood, toy, or craft shops
—Artists, writers
—Landscapers
—Photographers
—Home builders, remodelers
—Wild game farmers
—Flower and herb gardeners
—Fiber arts workers

just to name a few. For these, such old and now unused sites can become a gold mine of low-cost space or raw materials which can become the basis for a new, family-owned business.

NATURAL RESOURCES OF THE COUNTRYSIDE

There are endless natural features in the Dakota countryside which could be converted to cash, depending on the extent of one's imagination:

—Small lakes and ponds, sloughs
—Abandoned sand pits, quarries
—Native prairie grasslands
—Farmstead groves, wooded areas
—Rocky hills, buttes
—Sandhills, badlands, rough broken areas
—Pine, ash, cedar, oak, cottonwood

All these offer special materials and locations that can be converted to cash! There are hundreds of native plants, flowers, fruits, seeds, woods, grasses, stones, sands, clays, bones, fossils, and shells which can be made into hundreds of different products and into dollar income.

Who would buy such products? America is an urban nation now—whatever it may seem to us, looking across some of the vast and distant reaches of rural South Dakota. Many urban people long for a more quiet, simple life, such as they remember their ancestors talking about. A great many urbanites want to have a closer tie with nature and unspoiled, quiet places. Some want to be part of the "Old West"; they want to return "home," if even for a little while. So they load the kids in the minivan and come here or they buy bits and pieces of "here" by mail order catalog. Products such as you might produce can have great appeal to them.

FARMS AND RANCHES

It is common to hear farmers and agribusiness people say: "There is no room for the small farmer anymore...unless you have at least yea number of acres, you just can't make it." This may be true *if* you are going to compete in increasingly centralized production agriculture which demands high, increasing yields and larger and larger units of production. If that is what family farming means to you, it's true. But that isn't the only kind of farming there is. There are thousands of small-scale farmers making a good family living on very small farms and acreages, simply by looking at farming as being more inclusive than high volume wheat, corn and beans, and pigs and cows.

They have simply looked at a wider range of possible crops of plants, animals, and specialized products. Some of them are raising:

—Trees
—Nursery stock and seeds
—Vegetables
—Herbs
—Wildflowers
—Native plants and seeds
—Orchard fruits
—Firewood
—Florist supplies
—Mushrooms
—Wild fruits, nuts
—Cabinet woods
—Cereal grains
—Medicinal plants

just to name a few examples!

There is a growing market for many kinds of animals raised for food, stock, pets, game parks, zoos, and many other specialized purposes. They require a much smaller investment in land, equipment, and operational costs than ordinary livestock and often bring higher sale prices. Here is a sampling of possibilities:

—Dogs, cats, other pets
—Miniature farm animals
—Fish, bait animals
—Deer, elk
—Ostriches and emus
—Game birds
—Goats, sheep
—Buffalo
—Rare domestic livestock
—Rodeo stock
—Llamas
—Long-horn cattle
—Horses, ponies
—Native wild animals

There are many other possibilities. All these alternative plants and animals require some homework to learn how to raise, care for, and market them. One of the best ways to begin is to visit some of the many people here in South Dakota who are already doing it successfully. As with everything, there are many how-to publications available and organizations of people already in the business from whom much can be learned.

THEME VARIATIONS

There are lots of variations and knock-offs relating to plants, animals, or both. Many are possible that don't relate to using local resources but that could be started anywhere that a market can be developed:

—Animal motels
—Bakeries
—Marketing co-ops
—Dehydrated or frozen foods
—Pick-your-own acreages
—Specialty and ethnic cheeses
—Farm building storage units
—Corn, bean, or grain snacks

TOURISM, RECREATION, AND HISTORY

There is not a county in South Dakota, from Roberts to Fall River, that doesn't have undeveloped sites with interesting possibilities for attracting tourists and recreational visitors, who will spend money. Not all of these potential attractions are dotted along the interstate highways—and they need not be. Lots of tourists are especially looking for places that aren't. At home, they have had people and excitement up to here—they're looking for quiet places.

These sites include: locations of old military forts, trading posts, stagecoach stations, cattle and wagon trails, homesteads, sites of historic events, ghost towns, pioneer landmarks, and many, many, scenic locations and places of natural interest, like places to view wildlife, native plants, or fossil beds.

Many counties have sites with interesting stories of historic events recaptured that can add greatly to the appeal of visitors, in and out-of-state. For example, the people in Geddes, South Dakota, are developing an annual summer event based on an old fur trading post. Some stories have sufficient historical interest to be attractive for that reason alone.

Businesses that are possible in such settings include:

—Bed & breakfasts
—Ranch vacations
—Farm vacations
—Camp sites
—Hunting camps
—Gift shops
—Craft shops
—Re-enactor shows
—Tepee and cabin sites
—Nature walks and tours
—Fossil collecting sites
—Rocks and minerals
—Local history tours
—Native American events, exhibits
—Outdoor dramas
—Youth camps

If you aren't sure about where the sites of historic interest in your county are, contact your local or county historical society. Visit the local museums in your area. Talk to the folks who are active in these organizations. Or, contact the State Historical Society, Cultural Heritage Center, Pierre, 57501. Ask them about the points of historical interest in your county. Many counties and towns have histories recording the local past. There is a fair chance there is one for your county. Check the library or the local newspapers.

THE LOCAL ADVANTAGES

Using, or reusing, local materials can be a great advantage because there is such an abundant supply. Your costs for raw materials can be very low. You are not dependent on a distant supplier or a freight system, with their attendant costs. What you need is at hand, dirt cheap or free. This gives you a long leg up on production costs. Such local materials have a great intrinsic appeal to customers because they recognize them as familiar and related to their own experiences.

George S. of Minnehaha County has been taking down old farm buildings for years, to provide the natural weathered wood he wants to make picture frames, interior panels for homes, and a wide range of wood specialties. A bonus for

George is the antique iron hinges, hooks, and other hardware he finds in some of these old buildings.

The use of local materials has a positive appeal to tourists or persons living in settings far away simply because they *are* local, they reflect the areas they come from and they are real and not a look-alike fake.

There is wide interest in South Dakota and across the nation in all kinds of arts and crafts and skills that were a part of the daily lives of our grandparents. Things made by hand with simple tools and with knowledge preserved from the past have great appeal. Tourists like to watch artisans at work and happily buy their products. Here are a few examples:

—Pioneer arts and crafts
—Soap, candle making
—Furniture making
—Furniture restoration
—Hand tool making
—Pioneer machine restoration
—Wines
—Knitting, weaving, caneing
—Homemade ethnic foods
—Metalsmithing
—Wood specialty shops
—Leather and saddle shops
—Wild fruit specialists

There are a number of each of the above businesses scattered all across South Dakota, with many variations. There is room for many more. There is no foreseeable danger of flooding the market.

WOMEN'S ADVANTAGES

There are some service businesses in which women may have a real advantage. Often, they can be started with very little capital and they require the special knowledge, skills, or aptitudes that many women have from experience. Some of the following ones can begin gradually, without a full-time commitment and allowing time for other duties:

—Baking/decorating cakes for birthdays, weddings, anniversaries
—Planning theme birthday parties for kids and all ages
—Sewing formal dresses for proms, weddings, occasions
—Catering social events, receptions, weddings, parties
—Baking specialty breads, rolls, ethnic pastries
—Refinishing furniture and restoring antiques
—Caneing and fabric chair restoration
—Design of custom greeting cards, note cards

Often, it is a lot easier to build a business based on skills that are familiar, when equipment to produce products is readily available, and where there is an on-going demand for the products in the community.

NEW PRODUCTS AND SERVICES

Maybe the business you'd like to start has nothing to do with the use of local materials or local history. Maybe you want to offer new services in communication, or health or recreation or some other field that is really new, recently invented, on the cutting edge of what is fresh and exciting. Fine. Follow your dream. The processes for getting started are much the same. You may find you can do it in rural South Dakota.

CHAPTER III

HOW TO GET STARTED

WHERE TO BEGIN

Stop sitting on the fence! Just say "Yes!" Begin digging into the questions of running your own business.

In all cases, your first job is to get a clear idea of what you want to do. Do you want to make a food product and sell it through stores? Run a deer farm? Set up an office service business? Do you want to have a welding shop and build farm equipment? Do you want to raise herbs or flowers or run a gift shop? Or what?

Nail it down in plain terms. Don't stew about whether you think you can do it or not—just write it down so you can see for yourself if it is clear. And be honest.

For some people, writing it down is one of the hardest things to do in the whole process. Some folks just freeze up when asked to write down their plans. They stall. They delay. They hope it will go away. No one can force you to write it down, but writing helps to make it clear and makes it more real.

IS IT LOVE OR INFATUATION?

One of the important tests of your probable future success is: would you really enjoy what you are about to do? Did you choose it because you thought it might be a big money maker?

Is it something that is hot now, something people are talking about? How about four years from now—will they still be talking?

Do you know anything about how to go at it? If you don't know anything about the field, have never had any past interest in it, or paid any attention to it, the chances are you'd be best off to run the other way. In plain terms: don't start a business in which you've had no experience or know nothing about. Too often, by the time you learn, you will have wasted a lot of time and money—maybe too much and the Sheriff is just pulling up to the door. Learn about it first, before you jump in.

HOW ABOUT YOU?

Some important questions you may need to ask yourself:

—Is running my own business right for me?
—Do I have confidence in my own ideas?
—Will I listen to others' advice and opinions?
—Am I willing to take risks, not knowing if I will succeed or not?
—Do I have the health and energy to pull it off?
—Do I study the pros and cons of a new decision?
—Am I a self-starter?
—Can I make myself do things that I know I must, when they have to be done?
—Do I rely on others to decide things?
—Am I willing to work days, nights, and weekends to succeed?
—Am I willing to invest my own money, to give up things for self and family?

Asking ourselves questions like these is hard. We don't always like the answers we give ourselves! We don't want to be too hard on ourselves and give ourselves the benefit of the doubt. Still, most of us, down deep, know ourselves pretty well. And we know who gets hurt if we try to hedge or fudge or cheat on a test like this!

It's important to choose a business doing something you like and understand. The chances are very good that you'll do lots better, work harder, plan better, and be more successful.

WHY DO I WANT TO?

Try to be clear in your own mind as to *why* you want to start your own business. Is it because you like the kind of work involved? Because you know the field well and are good at it? Want to be your own boss? Want to work at home? Because you want or need more income? Do you want to create jobs for family or friends?

If you had your business up and running, where would you want to go with it? Would you want to build it up, expand, hire help? Leave it to your kids? Sell it? Would you want to work at it all your life? If not, when would you want to stop and get out of it? Would you want it to get as big as it could? Or only so big?

DO A TEST RUN

One of the best ways to get the feel of your proposed new business is to get a job in one like it or similar to it. You will get an inside education on what it's like. You will find out some things you hadn't thought of—and maybe, even some you would rather not know. You will have a much better idea of what you are getting into. And most importantly, you will be paid while you're learning.

Even if you have to work part-time or for free, just for the experience, it might be well worth your effort. Suggest to the owner that you are interested in the business and it won't cost much or anything to have you around. You will gain a lot of valuable information that will help you plan your future.

GO VISITING

It's quite possible that you can't find or get hired for a job in a business that resembles the one you'd like to start. So do the next best thing: go visiting. Check around in your region to find businesses that at least in some way resemble what you would like to do. If you possibly can, go talk to the people that work in them. Talk to the managers or owners. If you can do this, you will get a far more clear picture of what life is like, day by day, in such businesses. You will get a mental picture of what life might be like in a real, live business of this kind. What do these people do all day? What seem to be their main problems? What do they seem to be doing right and wrong? Usually, if you are honest with them, they will give you honest answers and opinions.

Don't settle for just one such business. Visit as many as you can. You will begin to see similarities in the answers you get to questions. Going visiting may be a lot cheaper and safer than setting up your own business, trying to learn in your own "schoolhouse."

If you aren't sure where the businesses are located that might be able to help, go through several of the phone books for the larger, regional towns in your area. Check the yellow pages. Ask the business owners if there is a state organization of businesses like theirs and how to find it. They may have a directory of names, addresses, phone numbers, e-mail, and fax numbers.

CHAPTER IV

HOW TO FIND THE INFORMATION YOU NEED

At some time or other, many of us have had ideas for starting our own small business. Many ideas are just passing fancies and don't last long, but some people have an idea that they just can't shake. It seems like it would work. It may even seem like it would be fun! The same idea keeps coming up and one thinks about how it might be set up and how it could work. Some people will carry such an idea in the back of their minds for years. Trouble is, that's where it stays. They never really *do* anything about it. So the years go on and the idea gets a little worn and old, never entirely forgotten, never really moving ahead.

REALITY CHECK

One of the best ways to find out if you're serious or not is whether you have enough interest to begin gathering information about your idea. Gathering information will include a lot of ways to proceed. It will include asking people about it—people already in it or a related business. They can help by giving you some insights from their experience. Ask anyone who might know more about your proposed business than you do: retailers, suppliers, wholesalers, salesmen, advertising and marketing people, distributors—anyone you can find who has had some related experiences. Some people are shy about asking for fear people will laugh at them. They don't like to appear dumb, and they're afraid their questions will show how little they know. But the test is this: if you aren't interested or curious enough to try to get some ideas on how your business might work, you are probably headed nowhere anyway. If you do try, and you find that what you have learned really interests you, and you want to know more, terrific. Keep on digging.

INFORMATION'S ROLE

Our era has often been described as "The Information Age." But information has been important in every age. Information can make the entire difference between success and failure in starting a new business, and, in keeping it going to produce a profit.

One of the biggest problems facing many new entrepreneurs is the lack of information they need to launch and test their business ideas. Far more serious, many of them don't really understand how to go about finding facts and information. While they should have learned this from their parents or in school, the sad fact is that this lack is one of the most serious failures of our educational system. And it isn't necessarily related to the amount of education or the number of degrees one may hold.

HOW TO BEGIN LOOKING FOR INFORMATION

First, get a clear idea of what it is you need to know. Define your question. If it is a complicated idea, you may need to write it down—or draw pictures or diagrams—to help you sort out your thoughts. Decide, and write down, exactly what it is that you want to know. You may not get it right on the first try. Keep at it until your written description says exactly what you want to know. There is a reason for taking the trouble to write it down. Ideas almost always look different when they are in writing. You can see them more clearly. You can see what you forgot to include or things you will have to begin to do, if you are serious about moving ahead. Don't let ideas just spin around in your head—write them down.

THINK AHEAD

Do your own thinking before you go hassle someone else. Try to break it down to the point where you can ask *clear* questions, so people will know what it is you are asking. If you aren't sure *what* it is you want to know, you haven't finished your homework yet. Sort things out until you *are* sure. That will help you to decide *who* to ask and *where* to look for answers.

One of the ways to uncover questions is to think through what it is you want to do, step by step. What is it you have to do first, before you can do what comes next? Do you know the kind of equipment you will need to do so-and-so? Do you know the kind of materials you will need—and where to get them—and their different grades and what they cost? Do you know what colors you want? And so on.

TWO OR THREE HEADS

If your own thoughts don't seem to make it all come clear, talk it over with family and friends. Often a person who is "outside" of your idea can look at it with a fresh view and help make the questions you want answered more clear. Make sure you know what your questions are before you start running in all directions.

WHO KNOWS?

This may be the most important thing you can learn about how to search for information: ASK YOURSELF: WHO WOULD KNOW THE ANSWER? Who, by nature of their work or their past experiences would have this information? Is there a group of such people? Where would I look to find them? Someone, somewhere, *does* know.

First of all, look for people who are engaged in the same or a similar business themselves, who have been over the road, who know the ins and outs, who knows where the bones are buried. No one knows more than the people who have been there. You may need to find those who will not see you as a possible competitor. You may have to contact people outside your immediate area.

SOMEBODY KNOWS

If you can't come up with the answer to Who would know?, ask yourself: who do *I* know, who might know who *would* know? In short, you become like a detective. You ask a lot of questions of everyone related to the case.

Most questions you will have can be answered for free or nearly free. As mentioned above, if you don't know who to ask, stop and ask yourself "Who knows more about this than I do?" Go ask them. They may not know either, but they can probably give you the names of people who know more than they do. Sometimes, things go along like this through four or five stages. You simply move closer to the answers you need with each step.

WHO ELSE KNOWS?

One can get lots of valuable help from the suppliers of the materials and equipment you may need. They, in turn, have learned from the experience of those whom they supply. Their help might include advice on how to set up a shop, how to ship goods, where you are most likely to sell and so on. It might well include any equipment you may need to operate your business. Who else knows? An important group is the wholesalers and retailers who will handle products like yours and sell them. Another group is the bankers and finance people who supply the capital and operating funds. They may have seen similar problems before, many times.

DON'T BE SHY

More often than not, the persons who know the most about a subject are those who are most willing to share the information. Real experts usually have no problem telling you what you want to know. They feel flattered that you asked. When you ask them, you show that you see them as an expert. Most people have enough ego so it makes them feel good to be asked questions. So, never hesitate to ask; the more famous, expert, and widely known the person is, the better the chances are that you'll learn what you need to know.

LIKE MINDS ATTRACT

There are very few products or services sold in this country for which there is not at least one trade association—sometimes there are a number of them. These associations are formed by people like yourself who are seeking information—answers to questions. The association staff and members can be a gold mine of information for you. They will probably have publications, how-to-do-it manuals, and books that contain lots of prior experience. They publish newsletters. They have committees of specialists that focus on specific problems within that trade or industry. Best of all, the association staff people are generally eager to help, for they may see you as a potential dues-paying member of their group. They hope to attract your interest. Be sure to track down your trade associations and ask for their help.

DON'T LOSE IT

Remember to write down what you learn as you go. Keep track of your information leads. You may have to go back again later with a different question. Use a small pocket notebook, for names, addresses, phone numbers, and names of places where you can find answers. Any bit of information that will help you find an information source or answer to your questions is valuable.

SEARCHING IS FOREVER

As you plan a new business, the quest for information, once begun, will never end. You will never escape the need to know more. There will always be questions ahead, no matter how successful you become. Decide now to learn how to find information. It's as much an attitude of mind as a process to be rote-learned. Our future success is directly related to the degree to which we learn how to find answers.

ENOUGH ALREADY

It is possible to gather too much information. Today new information is created faster than we can find or evaluate it. But we have to try. One of our biggest jobs is to learn to ask the *right questions.* How can we be sure which those are? They are the ones that enable you to move from where you are to your next objective. Some folks are nit-pickers and bean counters. They will delay taking action until the last scrap of information is in, however remotely related. They work so hard gathering all the facts, they never get started on the project itself. As a test, ask yourself: this fact is very interesting, but do I really need to know it *now?* What *do* I need to know *now,* to move ahead and make progress? Those are the right questions at any point in time.

PERSONAL LETTERS

One effective way to find sources of information is to write personal letters to people, organizations, and corporations who are related to the kind of work you plan to do. If you don't know the name of the person to write to, use a title such as "Director of Marketing" or "Production Manager." Failing all else, you can always address it to the president. You may be surprised that the higher up you go in the organization, the more likely you are to get a reply! And sometimes a really helpful one. But you must ask specific questions, such as "Where can I find a..." or "How should I go about doing...." You may come up empty but it never hurts to try.

THE LIBRARIES

Libraries are probably the most under-used valuable sources of information for new researchers. Libraries contain directories for many trade associations and industrial organizations. They have catalogs of periodicals and magazines. In your field of interest, no matter what it is, there are almost certainly one or more magazines, newsletters, manuals, industrial annuals, and other kinds of publications that may contain facts you can use. Libraries have encyclopedias, almanacs, and reference books of great variety. If your local library doesn't have what you need, your librarian knows how to direct you to another one that does and even to borrow it for you through interlibrary loan.

BOOKS AND VIDEOS

There are literally thousands of commercially-published, specialized how-to-do-it books and videos which give detailed instructions on how to start and operate various kinds of small businesses. While many of them assume that you live in an urban area (most people do, these days), they contain lots of information that can be applied wherever you are. And their costs are very low compared to any other way you could gather the same information. Some people are hesitant to buy a video or book that costs $25 or $30 that contains the information they could not gather themselves for hundreds of dollars. You will find ads for these publications in magazines on the news stands or listed in library directories of periodicals.

YOUR OWN LIBRARY

You shouldn't get too far down the road before you begin to establish your own personal library of materials relating to your business. It will include books and periodicals, and most importantly, items that you clip out of publications such as newspapers. Use file folders to contain the different topics so you can find them again and not lose them. When you see something in a current newspaper or magazine relating to your interests, clip it out and file it. Your files will grow rapidly, and pretty soon you will have a specialized library of your own.

COMPUTERS

Depending on the size and nature of your business, you may want to get a computer, if you don't already have one. If you don't, don't rush out and buy one until you are certain as to how it can help you. In a very tiny business, where you are the only employee/producer, you may not want or need one.

As you progress, suppliers will welcome the chance to bring you up to speed.

GETTING ON LINE

Depending on the nature and size of your new business, you may find very helpful information on the Internet. If you are into computers or have friends who are, post some questions on the Internet bulletin boards that relate to your interests. If you don't own a computer, try to find someone who can help with such an information search. If you don't know an individual, try your nearby public library or college. Having someone do a computer search for you may make lots more sense than investing in all the equipment you would need—not to mention the time it would take to learn how to do it yourself. There are thousands of Web site "Home Pages" that provide information and access to government agencies, private businesses, and non-profit organizations of enormous variety. It is possible that you could find information that you need fast and at little or no cost.

For the longer run, it is important that one get acquainted and comfortable with computers and their uses. The use of computers and varied related devices is growing at an explosive rate. In the business and everyday worlds of tomorrow, one will need to understand and be comfortable with these coming changes in order to operate at all.

KEEPING REAL

There is a lot of nonsense, hokum, and airheadedness which one has to fight through to arrive at a balanced and sensible role for the use of computers in the small rural family business. Too many people attach a special magic to having a computer, as if somehow storing information in one or keeping accounts with one makes the information more credible, important, or reliable than if it were written by hand. For many, computer ownership is simply evidence that one is in tune with the times, on the cutting edge. Computers are great for dazzling folks who don't understand how they operate or what they can and can't do. In addition to being status symbols, they can be great for obfuscating, bewildering, and giving weight to frothy data.

It is best not to be dazzled by the blinking lights. Ask yourself what it is you really need. Ask the equipment suppliers to convince you how and why you would be better off before you spend a bundle on the new hard and soft wares.

INFORMATION GOLD MINE

One of the largest sources of information—most of it free or at a very nominal cost—is government. All levels of government can be helpful: local, state, national, and international. There are literally thousands of people in government whose job it is to supply you with all information, data, and answers. How do you find out who they are and where they are? You ask! You ask the people in any local office nearest to you that seems to be related to what you want to do. For example, if you are interested in a business growing plants or animals or something related to them and you don't know where to begin asking questions, start with the "County Agent"—the Agricultural Extension office in your county. It's in the phone book. If they don't know the answers, ask them who might and follow through until you locate the right person. Another option is to write or call the Agricultural Extension Service at South Dakota State University in Brookings. Ag Extension offices at the Land Grant universities in neighboring states can be very helpful, too. Be sure to contact them.

This process extends to many fields besides agriculture. It applies to almost any small business. There are thousands of publications—booklets, charts, periodicals, reports published by hundreds of agencies of government, all for the purpose of supplying citizens with information. If you need help from a state or federal office, call the office of the Department of Commerce in Pierre or your Congressman here in the state and ask where to go for help.

PUBLIC ECONOMIC DEVELOPMENT AGENCIES

The State of South Dakota operates a number of offices devoted to helping small businesses get started and prosper. The Governor's Office of Economic Development (GOED), Pierre, offers a variety of services, mainly for larger businesses, that will create a number of jobs. There are people within the Department of Agriculture and some other state government departments that can offer help. There are federally-supported offices called Small Business Development Centers in Watertown, Aberdeen, Rapid City, Vermillion, and Sioux Falls, whose purpose is to help start-up businesses. The federal Small Business Administration in Sioux Falls offers a wide range of materials and services to assist small, new businesses. The SBA sponsors SCORE (the Service Corps Of Retired Executives), an organization of retired, experienced business managers and owners who give free advice and consultation to new start-ups as well as existing small businesses. Contact the SBA and ask if they can help you.

OTHER HELPERS

The Rural Electrification Administration (REA), as well as most investor-owned private utility companies actively seek to help new small businesses get started in South Dakota. Often, they can provide valuable technical assistance. They want to help because they realize that your new business may someday become a valuable customer.

COLLEGES AND UNIVERSITIES

Almost every college and university in South Dakota has a department of business or business assistance center that can assist you through consultation and research. Or they can tell you who can. Teachers in these colleges are often experts themselves and can direct you to other sources of information.

LOCAL ECONOMIC DEVELOPMENT COUNCILS/CORPORATIONS

There are about 140 local economic development groups, located in most counties and/or county seat towns, across South Dakota. They are mostly non-profit corporations made up of local people who would like to attract new businesses to their town or county. Some of them receive support from local government tax funds. These groups vary greatly in effectiveness and in their willingness to be of real help, especially if you are a really small and local business. Still, it never hurts to try. Ask local government officers (the mayor, county commissioners) if there is a development group in your area and who to contact. If you find one, ask them how or if they can help you get started.

LOCAL BANKERS AND LENDERS

Some local bankers are really interested in helping new small businesses get started. They will take a personal interest in helping you solve problems. Local bankers vary greatly in their willingness to help you with start-up questions. Some of them will expect you to persuade them that your venture has a prayer, rather than offering advice or help. Many local lenders confine their interest to the financial side of your business should you seek to borrow from them. Go visit your banker. Check him out. You soon will know.

GOVERNMENT LICENSES, REGULATIONS

No matter what the nature of your proposed new business, you probably will have to secure one or more licenses or permits to meet some kind of governmental regulations. You will probably need a sales tax license. If you plan to make, sell, or serve foods or drinks, you will almost certainly need to meet state and/or federal health regulations. The same goes for housing—motels, bed and breakfasts, and various outdoor camps. If you plan to raise money from investors or sell stock in your company to the public, there are state and possibly federal regulations. Check with the Department of Commerce in Pierre. There may be local zoning laws that relate to the locale of your planned business or in the placement of outdoor signs you'd like to erect. A good place to begin asking questions about possible government regulations is your local town hall or county courthouse planning office. They will be able to direct you.

HOW-TO BOOKS ON INFORMATION FINDING

As with almost everything, there are many good books outlining the process of finding information. One of the best recent ones is: *Finding Facts Fast,* by Alden Todd, a paperback published by Ten Speed Press, Berkeley, California. You nearest bookstore can order it for you. They can suggest other books too, as can your librarian.

All large bookstores selling new books carry how-to-do-it books on running small businesses. Be sure to check their magazine racks for periodicals that relate to your interests. You may be surprised to learn how much available information there is once you begin to poke around.

THE BOTTOM LINE

Always remember, when you have a questions: ask yourself "Who would know?" Go find that person. Be sure to ask him or her: "Who else would know?"

Chapter V

LOOKING AT YOUR REAL WORLD

GETTING REAL

Most of us know pretty well how to dream about the things we wish were so. As you dream about your new business, think about the people who could help you and what they need from you in order to be of help. Get a clear mental picture of what it is you want to do. If you want to operate a buffalo ranch or a specialized farm, lay out a plan on how it would be arranged and equipped. If you plan to produce clothing or a specialty food, make a model.

If you want to open a service business such as a bookkeeping service, day care, or mailing service, think of all the services you plan to offer and how they will work. Then, lay it all out on paper so you can see it and so you can explain it to someone else. No one can help you unless you can explain, step-by-step, what you are up to.

WHO WILL BUY MY VIOLETS?

If all the foregoing has gone well, and you can describe your product or service, you need to develop a profile of the people you think will be most likely to buy. Who will be your customers? Farm women? Kids? Hunters? High school girls? Veterans, car nuts, or someone else? If you plan to make kids' toys, who will be the likely buyer—grandparents? Get as clear an idea as you can as to who your customers will be. You can then begin to think about where they are and what you have to do to deliver the product to them so they can see it and buy it, wherever they may live.

Today, most products and services are designed with the buyer in mind. So, one needs to know as much as possible about them: how old they are, their level of income, where they work, how they think and live. A clear mental picture of your prospective buyers will answer a lot of questions for you.

MODEL BUILDING

If you are going to make a product for sale, you will need to make a model and probably several. You will learn a great deal that you need to know before you can go into production. What materials will you need? What kinds of fabric, wood, plastic, or metal? How much sugar, flour, and spice? How will you shape it and put it together? Will you sew it, glue it, rivet it, or what? What colors? In short, you really need to see it as you have dreamed it, to see how it looks and works.

LEARNING FROM MODELING

You can get a real education from model building. You will learn what works and what might be a better way to do it. You will learn about the equipment you will need to put it all together, the time it takes to make one, what size it should be, and what kind of work space you will need to build a lot of them. You can begin to see how it should be packaged, whether it be in a corrugated box, window box, or plastic shrink-wrapped. You will be very much smarter for having made a model, whether it is a kitchen apron or a tractor hitch. Until you have a model, you can't show it to anyone else and ask them what they think of it.

Modeling a service business works in the same way. Plan the steps you would go through, the space and equipment you will need, forms or printed materials you may need, and what actual services you will perform for people. Your model will allow you to see how you can strengthen your plan.

GETTING REALLY REAL

In business, you will become much aware of costs. Making a model will give you some ball-park idea of what it will cost to make your product, the cost of materials, the time it takes, the needed machines, equipment, and everything you need to operate.

THE STUFF YOU NEED

Make a list of the kinds of equipment, tools, supplies, and raw materials you will need to make your plan operate. Do you have an idea of where to go to get them? Will you have steady dependable supply sources? You can learn a great deal by visiting existing offices or shops of people already in business, as well as from equipment suppliers and salespeople. Track down the sources of materials you expect to use and make sure they can really be delivered when you need them.

HIRED HANDS

Maybe you can't build the model yourself because it's too complicated or you don't have the tools. So, you find a machine shop or a science lab or a food processor or whomever and make a deal with them to build one. Maybe you will need chemical tests or stress tests or something else technical. Maybe your area vocational/technical school or a nearby college such as South Dakota State in Brookings or the School of Mines in Rapid City can help. Help is probably not that far away. Ask yourself: Who *would* know where to look? Go find them. They may send you to someone else. So, you go find them. Keep going until you find the right one.

THE RIGHT ADDRESS

If you are setting up a store or public service office, you will want it to be as accessible and attractive as possible. It should be clean, fresh, and consistent in appearance with the products you are selling. Don't turn people away because it's dirty, messy, and shabby looking. Soap, water, and paint don't cost that much. People do judge by appearances.

If you are producing your product in a place where customers will never come, such as a kitchen, shop, or lab, practicality should rule. Clean, yes. Orderly, sure. But you can produce in your basement, garage, old store building, or anywhere your needs for water, waste disposal, and electric power can be met.

Everything else equal, you should start up business in the location that will cost you the least. If renting, don't agree to a lease that will take cash you need for other operations. You'll sleep better. Don't spend more than you can afford on appearances. You can do that when you get rich and have tax problems.

WHERE TO LOCATE

If you need a site where people can come to buy retail, you might elect to have them come to your home or garage or an outbuilding. If that doesn't work, take stock of the empty or rentable buildings in your town. Most South Dakota small towns have empty commercial buildings. Some may have been empty for a long time and may have some real problems, like leaky roofs, heating problems, bad plumbing, and just plain grubbiness. Don't trade low rent for too many of such problems; it might be a better decision to pay a little more.

Try to locate in a visible place, close to main traffic routes. Don't make it tough for people to find you or to describe your location. If you locate on a farm or ranch site, make sure there are directional signs.

TIME

There are a million reasons why you must take serious account of *time* in planning your new business. Here are some questions that help explain why:

—How much time does it take to make/build/offer your product?

—How many units of your product can you make in an hour, day, week?

—If yours is a service business, how many hours can you work at providing the service each week? 15? 25? 40? More?

—How much time will it take to clean up the shop, keep records, order supplies, make deliveries, work on sales and promotion each week?

—How much time off will you need for family, recreation, vacations, church and community work?

—Do you have any other job commitments that take time?

You can probably think of other questions besides these that relate to time. The important thing is to be realistic about the amount of time it will take to make the business happen. If you will be a one-person business where you will be the president, producer, marketer, and janitor, it will be very important to think through the whole operation, step by step, as to how it will all work and when you can do what. You will learn as you go along, of course, and make changes needed, but try to foresee as much as you can.

The forty-hour work week has been a standard in our country since the 1930s. If you launch your own business, plan to bid that idea goodbye. Studies show that the average entrepreneur works over 60 hours a week—and many, more than that. The good news is that these people state that they are happier than they were when they were working a 40-hour week for someone else.

PEOPLE VARY

People vary in the speed with which they can get things done. Some people can do in a week what will take someone else three months. Some folks simply freeze up if they have to decide "right now"! It's important for you to know yourself and move at your own pace. One of the great advantages of being your own boss is that you can do exactly that: you can move when *you're* ready. Be sure you plan carefully to fit your own style and peace of mind. Don't let the business start running you and being your boss. Decisions are made by you—not by the "business" or talkative friends, full of advice but with no experience.

FINDING BACKUP

If you know at the beginning that you are going to need help, try to get an idea of who is around who could be hired. Who could work with you—young people, old people, neighbors, or spouse? Can you find the help you know you will need? Can you explain exactly what you want them to do?

Most communities have some people who can work on at least a part-time basis. Senior citizens in good health are often very reliable and may welcome the activity. Many high school kids would welcome the income. Check with your senior citizen center and high school counselors.

Don't hire people until you really need them. It is far easier to hire people than to let them go. Don't even promise jobs until you are sure you can deliver. When you do hire, limit the number of hours at first. You can add hours later if needed. It's easier to add hours than take them away.

Be sure to keep good records of hours worked, rate of pay, and employment dates, since you may be paying withholding and unemployment taxes. Such taxes are not complicated, but you will need to get the necessary federal forms and be prepared to explain it all to your new employees. Contact the State Department of Labor in Aberdeen for more information.

In hiring people, as with everything else, be careful and cautious with your cash. In general, one probably should not be stingy in setting rates of pay, for people who are treated fairly—even generously—will be better workers. But operating funds disappear fast enough, no matter how hard you try, and it is well to be wary. Be sure you are meeting legal requirements on minimum wages. Check with the Department of Labor.

REALITY TESTING

Until you have an actual demonstration model or sample, it's almost impossible for people to know whether they like it or not, or if they would buy it or not, and at what price range. Price can make an amazing difference. So, whether you have a plan to set up a bookkeeping office or have a great recipe for cookies or want to sell costume jewelry, make or build some models or samples, keep track of your costs, and then begin to ask people (family, friends, neighbors, anybody who will listen) whether they would buy your product or service. Remember that people have very different ideas and tastes. If they like it, ask them why. If they think the service is needed, ask them why. If they're not very excited, ask them why. They may not want to hurt your feelings, but if you can, get them to tell you what they like or don't like about it. You may not like what you hear, but it is far better to learn what's wrong at this stage, rather than after you've already hired the hall and made a room full of products that no one wants to buy.

It's important to remember that your family or friends may not give you their honest opinion. They may feel they don't want to discourage you. Or they may want to avoid responsibility later for risks they feel you are taking. Even so, ask them anyway. You will learn something from it all.

This process is very important; don't skip it. Don't make the mistake of thinking that your product is so great that people will fight to get in line. One of the most important lessons you can learn in producing and selling is: LISTEN TO YOUR CUSTOMERS. Ask them what they want. Then, give them what *they* want, not what *you* want. It's their money. They are entitled to buy what they want. Any person in business who doesn't ASK HIS CUSTOMERS what they would like to have in goods or services is missing one of the greatest chances for success. It is simply astonishing how many sellers do not understand this simple truth. If YOU want to succeed with your product or service, ASK YOUR CUSTOMERS WHAT THEY WANT!

INVENTOR'S PRIDE

"Pride goeth before a fall," the Good Book says. It's so right. Inventors and people who come up with new ideas will often resist suggestions to change design, color, form, shape, taste, or whatever. It's so crazy: they want to sell, but they won't change to produce the thing that people want to buy! But realize that it's important to ask a large number of people. If most of them agree that you should change something, you'd better think about it.

CHAPTER VI

HOW TO PRODUCE AND DISTRIBUTE YOUR PRODUCT

HOW WILL YOU PRODUCE?

The first job is to write down the steps you will have to go through to produce your product or service. In short: write a recipe—a step-by-step how-to-do-it.

The recipe will show you what is needed and in what order: the space to work, the labor, equipment, and materials. The recipe will make it seem more real. Your recipe may also show other details, as the need for health and safety, inspections by regulators or other things not evident earlier. It will show the *time* necessary to produce each unit or batch and the numbers over a period of time—a day, week, month. Your how-to recipe guide will show you more plainly the cost of setting up shop, even on a very small scale. Depending on the nature of your product, you may have some real costs just to produce a model, which you will need to see what it looks like and what changes are needed in design, color, size, or other features.

Knowing what you really need by way of space and equipment makes it possible to begin to find answers: where can I get these items? How? Where can I set up shop to fit these needs? What's available?

Answers to such questions help to avoid buying equipment, renting space, remodeling, or whatever, before you are really clear as to what you need. Such mistakes happen far more often than you might think. People get excited and carried away and want to get moving. All they can see is dollar $igns down the road. They sometimes make tragic decisions and throw away money they have borrowed on contracts that won't deliver, leases that don't fit and equipment they can't use. They move too fast without doing their homework and they repent later.

In general, a rule of thumb: don't buy something until you need it, understand how it works and how it will help you.

ACTUAL PRODUCTION

There are lots of ways of going at the work of producing your product. You can do it all yourself, with you supplying the labor, running the machines, or doing whatever is needed to make the product.

You may find that you can buy many of the parts or ingredients that go into the product without having to make them yourself. Maybe you can buy most or all of them, and simply assemble them into your invention. You might be surprised how often this happens. Joyce W., who produces a meat sauce and other condiments, buys everything she uses in them and simply mixes the ingredients and packages them under her own label. There are hundreds of people doing crafts who buy all their materials in craft supply houses and put them together in their own way. Many farm machines and much of everything else we buy is built out of purchased parts. There are wholesaler and discount catalogs from which one can buy almost everything by mail. You will find their ads in the trade and special interest magazines. There are directories of manufacturers of everything under the sun, one of which is the widely known *Thomas Register of American Manufacturers.* You can get access to such directories at any large public library or from agencies who offer help to small businesses. Ask your librarian.

COTTAGE INDUSTRY

Many small businesses operate a kind of cottage industry, in which they farm out certain jobs to people in their community, who make the pieces needed and are paid for them on a piece-work basis, so much for so many. If you need lots of identical items, you might be well served to try this approach. And it allows the people who make items for you to work on their own time, at their own speed. This process does require you to be alert to quality variations between one producer and another. An advantage is that the money you pay them stays in your home community, and your producers will want to help you succeed in the business.

CONTRACTING

Some items you would like to sell may be too complicated for you to produce yourself. You may have to find a factory or laboratory that has the equipment and technical ability to do it for you. In such a case, you supply the specifications and they produce them for you at an agreed price, with your brand name or label. This is a very common practice.

SETTING UP SHOP

Sometimes, there is an advantage in setting up shop so that people can see for themselves the processes that go into making your product. If you are a craftsperson, a display of the methods by which you work, the tools you use or personal skills you display may have a lot of sales appeal. You can work in your home, garage, or any empty building. People will come to your shop to see you actually in operation. In such a case, you will want to design your shop to provide a setting appropriate to the work you are doing. You are part of what is being sold.

If you are producing a product in a setting which the buyers will never see or visit anyway, keep it simple. Keep it clean and reasonably respectable, for there will be some visitors, such as sales and delivery people. It is no disgrace to be poor as long as you are clean. Use the money you save by avoiding elegance and spend it on advertising and marketing. If you can sell your product, you can earn the funds to support your ego when you are richer.

CHECKING OUT THE COMPETITION

Early on, you need to learn whether someone already has something like your idea on the market. Are there any competitors? How do their products/services compare with what you have had in mind? Might yours be better in some ways? Cost less? Could it?

Try to learn all you can about your competitors—the people and their organizations. Who are they? Where are they? How big are they? How old? How creative? How aggressive? How do they produce and distribute? How do they go about marketing?

You can't possibly know too much about your competitors. There may be good reasons for the things they do, for they may already have had to learn the hard way. You can learn much from studying how your competitors operate.

IS THERE ROOM FOR YOU?

Try to learn something about the size of the market. How wide is the demand for products like yours? How often do people buy the product—and when and why? How many people per 100 or 1,000 will buy one? When? Is it a seasonal item? At what prices?

Someone before you came along had to go through all of this, too. There are good reasons for their packages/prices or other things that they do. In looking for information such as this, ask yourself: Who would know the answers to such questions? Go and ask them.

GETTING TO THE CUSTOMER

The methods of distributing your product or service will vary, depending on what it's like. If it's a service, like accounting, you have to decide whether clients will come to your home or office or whether you plan to work in theirs. In most cases, whether you offer computer services or hair styling, customers will probably come to your shop or office.

If you are making a product, it will matter greatly whether it is a food item, a garment, a bird house, a steel gate, or any of hundreds of other possibilities. If you intend to sell directly to customers yourself, you will need a small store or display space in your shop to which people can come. If you intend to sell through retail stores, you will need to be prepared to haul the product yourself or hire someone to do it, such as UPS or a freight trucker or US parcel post.

If you plan to sell by mail order, you will need space to store your products and a work space to do packing, packaging, keeping records, mailing cartons, price lists, labels, and everything else.

You might intend to sell mainly through public fairs, trade shows, seasonal events, or flea markets. That will require you to get some display equipment, tables, tents, banners, and probably a vehicle (van or pick-up) to haul your products and display equipment.

LARGER VOLUME PRODUCERS

If you expect to sell a larger number of your products in several counties, state-wide or beyond, you may need to set up agreements with wholesalers, and contracts with sales representatives, brokers, and jobbers. These people can arrange to get your product into the hands of retailers and onto the shelves in stores. Or they may help you to get space in mail order catalogs, on TV sales shows, or into many other possible systems. Distributors such as these work on commission, a percentage of which will vary with the nature of the product and the industry. Whatever the percentage you will pay, it will become an add-on to your costs and will affect your selling prices.

CHAPTER VII

HOW TO MARKET YOUR NEW PRODUCT

Marketing is an enormously important feature of your new business. By marketing, we mean what you have to do to get people to buy your product.

YOUR MODEL PLAN

It is important to realize that your marketing plans must come early in the game. The question is: If I had the product in hand, could I sell it? And if so, how? And to whom?

First, you must have already produced a product model. You may or may not have to make a batch of copies of the model that are exactly like the ones you intend to produce. Showing samples is the only way for your buyers to know what it is you have: what it looks like, what it will do, whether it really works as you say it will.

THE COMPETITION

Marketing comes before production because if the market isn't big enough for you to make a profit, you won't need to produce anything. To begin your marketing plan, you need to know your competition. You will want to know what the other products or services may already be on the market in which you will have to compete. So, hunt them down. Once again, check the stores and publications, visit retailers, wholesalers, salesmen, and others. Learn how these products compare with yours, both as to product features and the prices at which they are selling.

THE TOP REASON FOR SMALL BUSINESS FAILURE

It is common to hear that most small businesses fail because of a lack of money to carry them through until income from sales builds up. Have you heard that one? Wrong! Fact is, most small businesses that fail do so because of a *lack of a market*. Either there are not enough people or not enough people who wanted the product. Make sure you don't fall into the number one trap. Find out whether people will buy or not *before* you risk the family farm. Do your market testing.

TESTING

Once you have a model of your product—or a plan for the delivery of your services—it is important to *test* it early on, to see if people like it, want it, might buy it. *You* may love it and it may be everything you had in your mind's eye. But the real test is: will people buy it if it's on the shelf? To begin, one has to start with his family, relatives and friends. What do they think? Then, try retailers, salespeople who might have to sell it. Their opinion is important. Don't ask just one or two. See as many as you can.

TEST MARKETING

If your first surveys encourage you, make up a small batch of copies of your model/sample to be placed in a store, or sold however you plan to sell. If you're offering a service, plan your service package and try it out on some buyers. *You* need to see how things will go in the real world. Will anyone buy? At what price? Where and when? Market testing is a very important step: you must not invest heavily until you are sure that there is interest in your product.

Market testing will probably show you that you need to make some changes or improvements before the product goes on the market. Buyers and retailers may suggest some changes in size, shape, color, flavor, or something else. For example, poor packaging and labels can make or break you.

With the information you get from market testing, you can gradually increase the amount of product you produce without going out too far on a financial limb, before you really know what's going on.

GETTING YOUR PRODUCT INTO RETAIL SOURCES

To make a real-world test as to how your product will sell, you should get it on the shelves of stores that serve the general public, whether it's a grocery, clothing, hardware, or gift store. How does one do this? Well, common sense prevails: Go find the owner or manager and ask them if they will give your product a try. If it's a large store, call for an appointment to see the buyer of items such as you have. Be sure to have some samples with you, and be prepared to say what your prices are for wholesale, volume discounts, and such.

In general, there is no mystery in the process of getting into stores. Go and visit them and ask. If they have special requirements, they'll tell you what to do or who to see. And, remember, if they seem less excited than you are, it may be that they have already seen a half dozen other new products this week. And they may remember some that sounded great but bombed.

You should try to get into the largest stores with the most traffic. Putting your product in a really tiny store in a really tiny town may not tell you too much. Equally important is your ability to produce your product in large enough volume to keep the store supplied. This is really a headache for stores who may want to help new producers get started, but find, after they agree to put the product on their shelves, the producer wasn't able to produce fast enough to keep the store supplied. There is no use barking if you can't bite.

CHAIN STORES

In general, you probably aren't going to get far trying to test in chain stores. Very often their buyers are off in a distant city. Even if you go visit them or if they will accept a shipment of your samples to check out, they generally aren't interested until you already have a demonstrated track record in sales. And you really have to be prepared to deliver a large volume of your product on time, no ifs, ands, or buts. You probably won't be set up to do that until you're satisfied the product will sell. So, try to test in local settings that are manageable, which will allow you to start more slowly, at less cost.

FAIRS, FLEA MARKETS, TRADE SHOWS

You can get a sense of public interest in your new product at a low cost by showing it at public markets like fairs and flea markets. For one thing, people who come to such places are likely to buy on impulse if anyone will. They are looking for new and novel things. Your fee for booth space is relatively low and you have a captive group of potential buyers moving past you. Not all products are suitable for sale in these settings, so try to locate a trade show of the counterpart market for you product.

LACK OF BUYERS IN RURAL AREAS

If you live in a low population area and plan to produce your product there, you may have to set up a system to deliver your product to where there are enough people to make a market. That may mean hauling it or shipping it by carrier to retailers in larger places. Maybe it means you sell through trade shows and flea markets. Don't give up because you can't see many people out your kitchen window! Janet K. in Pennington County pays her brother-in-law to make two delivery runs a week in his van, to deliver her specialty food product. Do some planning to figure out how to get where the people are.

KIOSKS AND CART MARKETING

If you live near enough to a town that has a shopping mall or an active convention center, you might find a good marketing outlet with a kiosk or cart in the main public traffic courses. The mall or center may have lease units, or you may find that it will pay to own your own take-down unit. These kinds of sales venues seem to work best with a single product or small group of related products. They can be great for holiday-related products.

Carts and kiosks are good devices for testing potential sales, especially before investing more heavily in store space. They have great flexibility and portability.

MARKET TESTING A SERVICE BUSINESS

As a service business, you are essentially selling yourself and your ability to deliver quality, within acceptable time and cost limits. If you are starting from scratch, you probably will have to work for family and friends, to begin to demonstrate that you can deliver. The real tests come when you are dealing with strangers who are interested in you because of your knowledge and skills. There probably is no shortcut to simply persuading some starters to give you a chance—to test you out. If you can do well what you advertise and if there is enough customer potential, you can roll right on to glory. That is the test: are you any good at what you do and are there enough clients to keep you busy?

PACKAGING

Everything else being equal, packaging can make the difference as to whether buyers will pick your product off the shelf—or someone else's. Packaging should be bright, cheerful, colorful; it should attract attention and make your product stand out on the shelf.

If you've never done so before, go to a retail food or discount store and go down the aisles. Look at the shelves to see which packages catch your eye. Large corporations have spent millions to discover designs that grab customers. Ask yourself why they do. Color? Shape? Size? What?

Packages should have helpful information, give directions, contents. If it's a food, it must list the ingredients along with nutritional information.

TESTING PACKAGES

You will want to experiment with varied forms for your packages—whether it's a box, bottle, plastic bag, or shrinkwrap. Compare your package design with packages that are already on the shelf. Would yours stand out? Or will it get lost? Buyers have be able to see it to buy.

Once you decide what you want, visit your printer. If he can't handle it, he can probably suggest one who can. You need to talk to whoever is going to produce your package in order to keep costs in line. Your final decision will almost certainly be a compromise between what you would like and what you can afford, since your package costs will add on to your selling price.

Important: You should not let amateurs or your Aunt Marie design your package. You can have a great product inside an ugly or dull package and no one will buy. The wrong package can kill sales. Don't be careless and ruin everything with a bad package. Study the store shelves and get help from people who produce packages. They will know what's possible, at what price.

NAMING YOUR BUSINESS AND YOUR PRODUCT

Choosing a name for your product—and for your business itself—are very important decisions. Like packaging, names can make or break your whole idea. A good name ought to be clear, short, easy to spell, easy to pronounce, easy to remember.

A name can turn people on or off. It ought to sound positive. If it can describe the product or help define it, all the better. Don't be afraid to be creative and loose. Witness the names of popular detergents, cereals, soft drinks, and many other products.

Don't take the naming process lightly or simply grab one when you have to decide, as a sort of afterthought. Ask people for suggestions if you feel you need suggestions. If you have some names in mind, try them out on people. Think up a list of your own, and study the names of other similar products already on the market.

Try to find a name that is memorable and colorful. Above all, don't call your business "E & J Repair" or "Jack's Propane." Don't go goofy in the other direction either and call yourself the "Continental Consolidated Energy and Natural Resources Company, Limited," when you really aren't that big a deal. Remember that your choice of names is one of the most important decision you will make. It can help or hurt you.

REGISTRATION OF NAMES

If you choose a name for your business that is fictitious and not your own name, you will need to register the name you choose with your county Register of Deeds. For example: your name is Jack Jones but you name your business "The Rock Creek Trading Company." Go to your county courthouse, fill out a form, pay $5.00, and you are all set.

If you are setting up a corporation, you need to contact the Secretary of State. That office will do a search to see if there is already someone else using the corporate name you've chosen. And they will make sure that you don't include words in your name that might confuse or mislead people. For example, you cannot use the word "bank" in your name if you're not performing banking services, and so on. When all is clear, the office will issue you a certificate.

TRADEMARKS, PATENTS, COPYRIGHTS

There is a fair amount of confusion concerning these rights and the differences between them. They are completely different and they serve different purposes: They may be owned by an individual, partnership, corporation, association, or other collective group. Intellectual property is protected by:

TRADEMARKS:	on the name, logo, symbol, or design used on goods as a mark of identity.
PATENTS:	to protect rights to inventions or designs.
COPYRIGHTS:	to protect literary, musical, or photographic products.

These rights are issued to successful applicants by the federal government. If you plan to operate over a wide area, either through product sales or services, you may need to do a trademark or copyright search with the federal government to learn whether your material can be registered.

Patents require substantial time and expense to secure. For most small business entrepreneurs, they are of limited interest and may not be worth the effort.

Questions about these rights can be answered by contacting:

U.S. Department of Commerce
Patent and Trademark Office
Washington, DC 20231
Ph (703) 557-INFO

DESIGNING A LOGO

Logos are symbols to help people remember your product or service. Design should be simple, so it can be reproduced on your company letterhead or a 40 foot highway signboard without losing detail, impact, or effect. A logo should be timeless, not dated by current happenings or events. The longer you can use it and the more people who come to recognize it, the better it serves your purposes.

You may have some ideas of your own as to design, as may family and friends. But get a professional artist or designer to do the finished job for you. It will be money well spent. It will look professional and so will your product and company.

PRICING IS CRITICAL

Your product will sell only when the price is within a tolerable range, no matter how high the quality or the advantages it may offer. So, what is a tolerable range? How does one decide on price?

For openers, one has to know what is possible. You need to know what your unit costs are, to produce the product or to deliver your service. So, you will need to list the raw materials, wages and salaries, if any, the packaging, production equipment, and every other cost you can find involved in producing a sample batch of the product. For a sample you might choose ten items or 50 or any number that seems reasonable to give you an average per unit price.

Next, add in your fixed costs, (those costs you incur as a result of being in business at all), such as rent or space costs, insurance, taxes, regular on-going utilities such as phone, electricity, and all other costs that go on, month after month.

Next, add any costs you may have for moving your product to market. These could include costs for freight, mail, UPS, or other means. If you deliver them yourself, you will have to add on costs for your vehicle.

Finally, if you plan to sell through a sales representative or broker, he will want a commission which could run from five to twenty-five percent of your selling price, as a ball park estimate. And he, in turn, has to sell to a retailer who will add on his profit or "mark-up" to finally arrive at the price the customer will pay for your product at the store. Retail mark-up can vary greatly too, from less than 10 percent up to double your wholesale price.

To arrive at production costs, decide how many units of your product you will make in a fixed time period, such as a week or month. You can pro-rate the share of the costs to be assigned to each unit for the time period.

PRICING SERVICES

If you plan to operate a service business, you will probably charge an hourly rate for your services. To arrive at that hourly rate, you need to add up your fixed costs (space, utilities, etc.) and expenses for materials, equipment, contracted services, or whatever you need to do specific jobs. To this, add your profit (the amount you want to earn above all your actual costs). The total will give you the hourly charge.

Just as with selling goods, you need to use judgement as to what the traffic will bear and what comparable service businesses are charging to set your price.

WHO PAYS YOU?

Many beginning producers do not include their *own* time in their labor or production costs. Often, this may be necessary to get started and keep operating costs down. A good rule of thumb is: don't take out money for yourself until your profits will cover the amount you draw out. That will keep you real. But, presumably, you are starting the business in order to increase family income, and your time has value. So, early on, you should plan to add in the costs of your own time devoted to the business. Pay yourself a wage or salary, however small. You can increase it as the business grows.

QUESTION BEFORE THE HOUSE

The big question is: can you produce and deliver your product at a cost that will allow you to make a profit? By adding up all the costs you can identify, you will have a fairly accurate idea of the amount of money you will need to recover from sales to break even.

Estimating your price per unit or per hour of your time for services will allow you to estimate how many units you have to sell to bring in a gross profit of, say, $1,000 or $5,000. And since your net profit per unit will be only so much, how many so-muches will you need? Could you produce that many? Could you sell that many?

MOMENT OF TRUTH

Is your estimated retail price in the ballpark, so far as the competition and common sense is concerned? Most first price estimates are too high and so one has to go back over the costs to find out what can be trimmed, made more efficient or cut out. Your product may be worth a high price, but if it's too high it will make the customer uneasy and may turn him away, especially if he's never seen or heard of your product before. You probably will have to keep your prices within ranges being charged by your competition, at least until your product is a proven seller and is established.

AN INEXACT SCIENCE

Pricing is not an exact science. After figuring all your costs to produce and deliver the product to a point where the customer can buy it, common sense, intuition, and the advice of experienced people who sell for a living will have to be considered. Then, at that point, you simply have to decide, put the product up for sale and see what happens. Since pricing is only one of the factors that govern sales, it is very important that your entire effort is not stopped in its tracks by a dumb decision on pricing.

CHAPTER VIII

ADVERTISING AND PROMOTION

No one can buy your product or service until they know about it and where to find it. Yet some people will spend hundreds and thousands of dollars to get set up—for working space, equipment, raw materials, hiring help—doing countless things to get into business, without any serious planning for advertising and promotion. And some people go goofy in another direction, spending on promotion of a product with no market testing for salability.

SINE QUA NON FOR SUCCESS

Promotion is often undervalued, sometimes fatally so. After all of your efforts to design and produce your product, it's dumb to lose everything because buyers don't know it exists. It is hard to overemphasize the importance of advertising and promotion. It is difficult to get too much of it.

Some people really believe they can't afford to advertise. Fact is, they can't afford not to, and they often learn this the hard way. Advertising can be a black hole so far as money is concerned. The task is to learn what is possible on a small budget. There is much that you can do with very little money, once you learn how. You may need help on this from experienced people, both in business and in advertising.

Plans for advertising and promotion often wait until last, when the product is up and running and being manufactured or the service is being offered. Then the owner comes face to face with the idea that he needs some customers. Often, by then he has spent more than he planned on getting everything else ready. So the prospect of spending more money on advertising seems scary. Maybe he should wait and see how things go. Maybe people will discover it and buy it anyway. Don't bet the farm. The reality is they probably won't. The reality is you probably can get the advertising and promotion you need at a cost you can afford. Get help on how to do it and place it where it will do the most good, at costs you can live with.

WHO CAN HELP ME?

Ask yourself what similar small businesses do to get themselves or their products known. Make lists of what they do. If you know some business owners, ask them. What do community groups do when staging public events? How do they get visible? What do they do that you could adopt, change, or modify for your purposes?

WHERE TO BEGIN

The first question is: Who do you want to reach? You need to get a clear picture of who your possible customers are and where they are, what they are like, how they live, and as much descriptive information about them as possible.

Next question: What do you want to tell them? What is it that you want them to know? Why does your product meet their needs or wants, why is it unusual or different or better or unique? And, you want to tell them where and how they can buy your product.

GETTING HELP WITH PROMOTION

More heads are often better than one. Ask people to help you with promotional ideas and decisions. Start with your family and friends. Talk with the advertising managers at local newspapers and broadcasters. There may be a teacher of journalism or advertising in a nearby school or college. Get some book and manuals from the library—or buy them, with help from book store managers. Contact trade associations that are related to your project and ask them for help. And: study, study, study, the ads of your competition. Buy magazines and papers in which similar businesses advertise so you can see what they are doing. Buy trade and special interest magazines for a really low-cost education.

PROMOTING THE SERVICE BUSINESS

When a service customer buys your services, he is, in essence, expressing confidence in you and those who may work with you. That means you need to become known and acquainted with the people who make up your customer pool. Early on, you have to decide on the size of the radius in which you will offer your services. If you are willing to travel, how far? That radius will define the arc in which your future customers live. You odds in getting service contracts and/or walk-in business are greatly increased by the number of people who have met you, seen your picture, heard you, and feel they know you. As in politics, name recognition is important. When they need help in accounting or a hair-do or a new transmission, they'll call you. So, you have to get out among the public. Go to stuff. Attend. Advertise with "business card" ads unceasingly. Volunteer. Join. In the service business, you are selling you.

ABSOLUTE MINIMUM NEEDS

No matter how tiny and poor your business may be, you need at least these things:

+ Business Cards—to be handed out freely. Include them in mailings, and in every purchase package. Leave them around in public places, everywhere.

+ Small Folder/brochure—one that will fit, perhaps folded, in a number 10 business envelope, which explains your product or service and your strong points. This can be a self-mailer, requiring no envelope.

+ Business Letterhead—an attractive letterhead can help create your image and build confidence in your business.

+ Labels, Tags—if you are producing a new product, you will need labels on packages, containers, no matter how modest or simple. Tags can be a powerful sales aid, telling where, how, and by whom something was made. They can be used to say why the product is special or explain its history. They can stir imagination and emphasize quality, and they are low cost.

+ Outdoor signs—You will need a sign at the site of your business that is readable from the road so that people who come looking for you can find you. Depending on the nature of your business, it should be clear, neat, and a little larger than you might feel is appropriate. (If you slop some paint on an old board, that is about how folks will think you run your business, too)! If you are offering a professional service for which you would like to build some measure of dignity and standing, you can have a more sedate, professional-looking shingle-type sign. Whatever: be sure you have signs. And be sure your street number or address is large enough to be read from a passing car.

Depending on your setting, location, and type of business, you may want highway and directional signs out and away form your business location, as far as you can afford to have them. You may need county or state permits for these. One is reminded of the legendary Wall Drug Store signs all across South Dakota and the world. These signs have been a model for many other businesses everywhere. They work.

LOW COST/NO COST PRODUCTION

Depending on the size and nature of your business:

+ Print handbills (like small auction bills) on newsprint; put them in all possible public places. Kids can help.

+ Use small cards, the size of color postcards, for your message and for insertion in literature racks at tourist stops.

+ Get fabric signs and banners you can re-use for hanging at fairs, flea markets, trade shows, and the like. Remember balloons.

+ Volunteer to speak or set up displays at area civic and service clubs, church events, local fairs, trade shows, and cultural events.

+ Print large posters on newsprint or butcher paper or other low-cost stock.

+ Packages, cartons, wrapping paper: when you can afford it, have them printed with your name, logo, and promotional messages. Use colors where you can.

+ Adhesive Stickers: use on outgoing mail, windows, package labels, and so on. They are low cost and have many uses.

GETTING INTO PRINT

- Find the people in your community or area who are writers or ad people for area newspapers; journalism teachers in area schools, and in larger areas, advertising managers. Ask them how you can get stories published about your business in local papers, trade papers, company and community newsletters.

- Call news and features writers for area media. If you can't find them, ask the media for names. Get some books and manuals on promotional news writing at your library or book store and bone up.

- Plan occasions in your store, shop, or factory which can result in news stories. Observe holidays, have sales, open houses, recognition days, contests, raffles, giveaways, and other similar events.

- Television news is increasingly filled with novelty and entertainment features. Contact the local station news director or anchor and tell them about your business. You may get invited on to describe what you are up to. TV is a very powerful medium, worth the extra effort.

- Economic development offices are always eager to learn about new small businesses. These include government offices, chambers of commerce, and utility service offices. They will publish stories about you in their newsletters and send out releases to the public media. Contact them and ask them to help you.

BASIC LAW OF THE PROMOTIONAL JUNGLE

Repetition. That's it. Repeat and repeat and never stop! Don't buy one or two ads and then say, "I advertised but it didn't do any good." This is a very common mistake. It is no accident that some companies in this country are household names. They keep at it, endlessly, because they know they must. Dave T. ran a classified ad in a Miner county weekly for 40 years! Everyone knew what he was selling!

RURAL VALUES

Sometimes, rural people are naturally shy, modest, and retiring. Promoting themselves and their products does not come easy for them. They are embarrassed by tooting their own horn. They feel it is somehow unseemly to push oneself forward, to attract attention. If this sounds like you, work to overcome it. If you feel that you can't and will never have the touch, then by all means get help from someone who can do it and who knows how.

PAID ADVERTISING

If you don't know how to lay out an ad, or how they get put together, study the ads of competitors and other similar companies. They have been over the road. Ask yourself why they arrange the space and say what they do in ads.

When you are paying for ad space in public media, you should expect and get help from the media advertising and sales people. Most of them will welcome questions and will volunteer to help. Make a list of the things you would like to tell people about your product or service. And think hard about what your future customers would like to hear about your product.

AD AGENCIES

If your new business plans to sell statewide, over a large area, or to specialized markets, you should probably head for advertising agencies. You will need their help to place ads in large coverage media. Their specialized knowledge can save you money and give you a fast education by working with them.

WHERE TO FIND INFORMATION

As with all other aspects of your business, you can learn about advertising at your public library and at bookstores. There are books on how to promote almost everything produced in this world. Ask your librarian, bookseller, and the local advertising people what is available that could help you. You can buy a how-to book on low-budget advertising for less than the cost of one display ad or broadcast spot in your area media.

CHAPTER IX

HOW TO MAKE A BUSINESS PLAN

GETTING INVOLVED

Most people who start a new business have been told or have read somewhere that they need what is called a "business plan." There are some differences between what the average person might consider to be a plan and what is contained in a business plan. We will look at a simple business plan below.

Planning—or the lack or it—can make or break you. Most small businesses that start and go broke do so because of a lack of planning. In a new start-up, nobody wants or plans to lose. They lose because they *don't plan* carefully enough. Large numbers of small businesses fail because they don't have enough capital to launch *and* stay open through the first tough months. Probably more fail for the lack of a market: there simply weren't enough people who were interested in their product and they didn't check that before they launched. If there had been good planning, some of these businesses would never have started in the first place; the plan would have shown that it wasn't going to fly.

CLEAR THE AIR

Planning means *written* plans. Nothing makes an idea come clear faster than laying it out on paper. Aspects of the project that were not clear before jump out at you. It simply is not possible for most of us humans to keep all the details clear in our heads alone. We forget. We pay the most attention to those parts of the program that we like the best (like to produce, hate to sell). We will even avoid thinking about the tough or most difficult parts of our plan.

Basic to planning is to be able to describe what it is you want to produce—or how you hope to serve. What is it for? What will it do? What will it look like? How will it work? How will it be different or more attractive or better? Unless these questions can be answered, it can't be built and it can't be sold and there is no use going any further. Get a clear idea of what you want to do.

A written plan can help you set goals so you can check your progress and lay out your future directions. No matter how small your business, make a plan of what you are going to do, by when, and with what effects.

THE TINY FAMILY BUSINESS

No matter how small your proposed business will be (where you are the only employee as well as president and janitor), it is important to put your plan on paper, even if you are the only person who will ever see it. It will help you to get things done in the right order, remind you of things you might otherwise overlook or postpone. If your family or friends are going to put money into the business, they are entitled to see the plans for it. It will help insure that everyone understands what's coming. Your plan will allow you to set dates for completion of this or that and will clarify your thinking and help you to see why some things may work and some won't.

PLANNING A LARGER BUSINESS

If you are planning a business that will require you to look for investors, seek loans from banks or other lenders to help cover an investment in work space, equipment, marketing, and payroll, you must prepare a business plan. No responsible bank loan officer or any seasoned investor is going to loan you a nickel unless you can provide a written plan of what you are up to. These folks may be a tough sell anyway, but they certainly won't budge without details and disclosure of what you plan to do. They will want to see how you hope to earn some income which will offer them some blind hope that you will be able to pay them back.

ORGANIZATIONAL OPTIONS

How your business will be organized or structured can have an important effect on how it succeeds. Otherwise careful plans can get upset without a thought-through decision on the following questions:

+ Will you go it alone or will there be other people in the business with you? If others, who? Family? Friends? Persons who can contribute in some special way?

+ If you expect to have other people with you, ask yourself, "why?" What will they do or how will they help insure success?

+ If there will be others, how well do you know them? Are you certain that you can get along with them? Why do they want to be a part of the business? Was it their idea or yours? Are you certain that you are agreed on plans?

+ If there will be others, who will be boss? Will they be partners, either more or less equal? How will the work be divided? How will they share in the profits—and the losses, if any? Do they have the personal qualities to stay and stick it out?

+ Will you set up a sole proprietorship or a partnership or a corporation in some form? You will need an attorney to draw up the papers.

CHOOSING AN ORGANIZATIONAL STRUCTURE

Plan to give careful study to the kind of organizational form you adopt for your new business. If you are alone in the enterprise and expect to operate it yourself, you probably will do so as a sole proprietor. That means you would be responsible yourself for everything in the business, receive income and pay bills and taxes yourself. You are the sole and only boss.

It is not unusual for two or more people to invent a business together, over time. Often, they are more interested in the nature of the business and how to produce their product than how to organize the business. And often, they end up in a partnership. Partnerships can be fine, as long as the partners are very clear with each other in the beginning, as to the duties of each and who will handle what part of the business, how decisions will be reached, and so on. If one is not careful at the beginning, partnerships can go sour later on because of disagreements and misunderstandings. If you plan a partnership, be sure you have a written agreement on how it will work.

Corporations offer some advantages in the ways ownership is shared, how profits and losses are handled. They can provide a shelter against personal liability which can be helpful. Corporations are entities in their own right before the law, somewhat like individual persons. They can do nearly everything an individual can do, such as own property, acquire debt, be taxed, and so on.

YOUR BUSINESS PLAN

Over a long period of time, people who own, manage, and finance larger businesses have developed a form for presenting information about a business operation which is more or less standardized. This form is called a "business plan" and is the accepted pattern in which loan officers, business managers, investors, and finance people expect to find this information.

The following outline suggests a form for the information that an investor or banker will want to see. Not every item in the outline will apply to every plan or business. A very small business might have a plan which would include information under all the major headings but in far less detail than the outline suggests.

The production of a business plan as described in this outline takes considerable time and effort, but it is a necessary step to complete if you are seeking serious money through loans or investment funds. If you are planning a larger business, you should have a detailed plan, whether or not you need to borrow funds, just to keep you on track and to test your progress.

This model is intended to serve as a guide only. Changes in this outline will be required to fit individual businesses. Common sense will have to guide the amount of information that can or should be included.

BUSINESS PLAN OUTLINE

I. *Summary.* A brief description/digest of the detailed information in the plan. One or two pages.

II. *Description of the industry or field of service.* Include nature, size, characteristics, growth rate and potential, problems, principle operating organizations, site of markets, needed facilities, changes foreseen, government regulations that may apply.

III. *Description of the company.* Include the name, legal form, date, location, address, phone, and computer numbers, liaison/contact person, ownerships and percentages of ownership, nature of capitalization, cash or property.

Description of the business in detail: What it will do, how it will operate, the goods or services it will offer.

IV. *Products/Services.* Include detailed descriptions of products or services: facilities, equipment, materials, employees required to produce them, availability of each, costs for each, broken down in detail, legal requirements or special requirements; any special problems relating to the enterprise in product/service production.

V. *Marketing/Sales.* Include description of customers: who they are, where they are, characteristics, size of customer groups; geography of proposed markets, customer areas for primary and future possible sales, growth potential.

Prices for product/service sales, product mix/variety of items, market share to begin and through growth, rates of growth, dollar volume, terms for sales, contracts, agreements, sales methods and organizations, costs for sales.

VI. *Management.* Include: who are the key managers, resumes, job descriptions, compensation, who are the board of directors, resumes, stockholders, percent held by each, how received, by cash or in kind, reasons why management is capable.

VII. *Finance.* Include: present financial statement, financial statements for prior years (2-3) if any, projections for next three years, to include cash flow, profit and loss, balance sheet, schedule of salary and benefits for management and officers, leases, rentals, working capital, debts, assets.

Include uses to which proceeds from loans would be put, why loans are needed, terms for repayment. Include methods of accounting to be used.

VIII. *Legal.* Include articles of incorporation, partnership agreements, by-laws, information on licenses, agreements, contracts, insurance of all types, stock issued and to whom, agreements governing stock transfer, stock rights. Include: names, addresses of attorney, accountant, banker, others.

IX. *Other.* Include statement of risks and assumptions, building plan time schedules, other supporting data.

Many people who plan to start up small businesses are not familiar with the accounting procedures that go into the makeup of financial statements usually contained in a business plan. To prepare the financial statements, it may be necessary to get a local accountant to help prepare this material, especially the cash flow statement, profit and loss and balance sheets. Financial projections for several years ahead may seem difficult but they provide the best estimates possible under the plan and are based on projected income from sales, estimates of volume and like figures. Figuring them out provides an important test of the soundness of the plans developed for the business. If the financial statements are a problem, find an accountant to help with them.

Disclosures in the business plan concerning the legal arrangements for the business help to provide insurance that the needed documents, agreements, contracts and such are actually in place. Larger, complex plans will require an attorney to help supply this material.

CHAPTER X

WHERE TO FIND START-UP MONEY

START-UP MONEY NEEDS

Because of enthusiasm about the product itself and hopes for its success, thorough planning about the detailed costs of getting started sometimes gets overlooked or downplayed. For example, a serious oversight can be the failure to include funds to support the business operation during the early months or years, before the business begins to return a profit.

The following checklist may at least help to focus on the funds needed to go. Add up the probable costs of:

—Finding and remodeling location
—Rents and utilities
—Equipment and supplies
—Salaries and withholding
—Production costs
—Taxes and insurance
—Licenses and permits
—Packaging
—Packing and shipping
—Sales and distribution
—Advertising and promotion
—Travel
—Legal and accounting services
—Signage and printing

A good rule of thumb: estimate your expenses high and income low. It helps to avoid problems later. Your totals won't be exact, of course, and you may not need to include all of the above categories. You may need to add some of your own. The result will help it all to become more real.

Be sure to include funds to operate the business during the start-up time to cover expenses before you receive any income back from sales. It will vary greatly depending on whether you/your family have other sources of income to provide living expenses. Operating expenses begin on opening day. You should probably plan on running the first year with expenses exceeding your income. This is a very critical time for many new businesses: they can't survive the time period between launch and break-even. Make early plans on how you will handle it and survive.

A LOOK IN THE MIRROR

Do you have enough start-up funds of your own or within your family? How much could you raise within your family? Will you need to borrow somewhere else? *Could* you borrow, outside the family? Do you have existing debts, such as large amounts on credit cards, retail credit purchases, education loans, home mortgages, car loans, or other major debts? Do you have property you could put up as collateral for a loan, to list for security? Borrowing means having to pay back, and that means including loan payments, with interest, in your monthly operating budget.

Many people assume that they will need to make a loan before they can start their new business. The only way to know for sure if you will have to borrow is simply to sit down and do your homework. Do some hard thinking on what must be bought and paid for and what can be done without. No shortcuts on this one. Asking the advice of others who have already been there and done that is helpful. Finally, it will depend on what *you* will be able to do and how you will go about running your business. Doing this ahead of time is lots less painful than trying to pick up the pieces later. Borrowing is not a requirement of starting a business. There are people who plan carefully, make-do creatively, and avoid it. If you don't have to borrow, don't. It takes off a lot of pressure.

TIGER TRAPS

One dangerous sinkhole for losing money is the office location and equipment. Fresh, new, and handsome is nice to have and gives the appearance of being successful on opening day. But ask yourself what is really needed. In the case of office equipment ask yourself exactly how you will use it and why you need it at all. If you buy, consider used and second-hand equipment. Many people avoid used equipment out of fear of large repair bills. But often you can pay for a lot of repairs for the difference in savings between the new and used price. Very often, you can win with used equipment and save a bundle.

LEASING

Leasing is a concept you should take seriously. These days, one can lease almost anything: office/shop space, equipment, vehicles, services. Leasing can greatly reduce start-up cash needs. It avoids property taxes. It avoids many maintenance costs. Leasing avoids problems of disposing of obsolete or no-longer-needed equipment. Give serious thought to what you can lease instead of buy.

HOME-MADE SAVINGS

Can you build it yourself? Items like shelving, storage, counters, and work surfaces, containers, supply racks, and partitions are examples. Sometimes, it is possible for the owners and friends to build items of production equipment as well, with immense savings in start-up costs. If you can't build it yourself, maybe there is a craftsman nearby who can build it for you, at real savings over factory-produced new equipment.

START-UP MONEY SUMMARY

Doing your homework on money estimates means doing a through run-through on what you propose to do in your business. What is the product or service you will offer? How much will it cost to produce a unit or offer the service, including equipment, supplies, and everything that goes into it.

To whom will you sell the product? How many will you hope to sell? How many can you produce and how fast? What will you charge and what will be your profit on each unit sold? Will you sell direct, wholesale, retail, or how? What will it cost you to put this whole process into motion?

You need to have the best estimates you can get before you can know what you need in start-up funds. You need these estimates before you try to borrow from anyone.

What is the difference between your costs to produce and the price at which you will sell a unit? Does a profit look possible? How many units or services must you sell to break even, so that your income will cover your expenses? If you plan to borrow, you must know, because the lender will ask.

By now you should have at least a ball-park idea of how much money you will need and how much of it you can furnish yourself. You will know if you need to borrow. You will have learned about the amount of sales you will need to show a profit. You have to have this information; don't try to leave home without it.

DO NOT PANIC OR DESPAIR!

If you find that the amount of needed funds is far beyond anything you had supposed, don't give up! Take a harder look at the amounts you included in the various categories of expense. Re-check your equipment costs. Ask yourself what you absolutely must spend. This process is simply a part of budget-building—you will be doing it all the time in the future, running your business. So, begin looking for ways you can save, cut back, be more efficient. Don't spend money if you can avoid it. Dollars disappear like magic, even under a vigilant eye.

YOUR OWN INVESTMENT

Take a realistic look and make a decision on the question of how much of your own or family funds you can invest in your new business. Do you have savings you can spare? Can you borrow on your home or car or other property? Give some thought to what you would do if you lose it all. Putting your family financial future at risk may be too great a danger.

TIME IS MONEY

Don't discount the amount of time that you have and will put into the planning and setting up of your new business. While you may not be able to convince possible lenders that your investment of time has a particular dollar value, some record of it may help to impress them of your seriousness of purpose and commitment to starting your new business. They will understand better that you really mean business.

GOING TO THE BANK

Bankers and other lenders make loans because they expect to get their money back again, with interest. Interest is the rent you pay them for the use of the money. Your banker will want to know how much of your own money you will put into the project. He knows that if you have some money of your own involved, you probably will work hard and be a better manager. He will want to know about your personal and family financial condition. He may ask you for a statement of your family assets, that is, any property you own, savings and so on.

The banker will ask you whether you have property or assets that you are willing to pledge as security for your loan.

If you have no money to put into the business and little or no property for collateral, your chances of getting a loan are probably very slim. The banker isn't being a greedy old scrooge. He simply needs to have some assurance that you will ever be able to pay him back.

FINDING BACKUP

If you have little or no collateral of your own, your lender may ask if you have a relative or friend who could co-sign the loan agreement with you. That means if you can't pay back the loan, the co-singer agrees to do it and to stand behind you, for backup.

Your relatives or best friends may not be all that eager to co-sign a loan with you. Maybe they can't afford the risk, if you go broke. Maybe they feel that you haven't done a careful enough job of planning. They may be less sold on your idea than you are. So, you should be prepared to explain your plans to a co-signer in the same amount of detail that you would to someone who doesn't know you at all. It's only fair to them.

GET REAL

People who don't know how much money they really need or how they plan to spend it, aren't going to get a loan. Your banker/lender will want to know exactly how much money you would like to borrow and what you plan to use the money for—what you will buy or how you plan to use it. He is not just being nosy. He is just checking on how carefully you have done your planning. He will feel that if you don't have a clear idea of how you will spend it, you probably don't have a clear idea of how you will pay him back.

Above all, don't ask for more money than you need. Don't round it off to the nearest five hundred or five thousand. Don't try to slip in a little extra to pay off your credit card or pick up a new fishing rod. Be able to explain and justify the amount you request. The less you borrow, the easier it is to pay back.

WHAT GOES AROUND...

Your bank/lender is going to ask you when and how you plan to pay the loan back. He will want you to explain. You would, too, if you were loaning the money. If your answers aren't clear, no loan. Your family or friends may be easier to convince and ask you fewer hard questions but they shouldn't, because they aren't doing you or themselves any favor.

Some lenders, including banks, may put some restrictions on how you can spend the money you borrow from them. They may say that the funds can only be used for certain purposes and may not be spent however you might wish. They are simply trying to make sure you don't get into a financial hole you can't crawl out of. Don't get mad at the banker if he suggests how he thinks you should use the money. Remember, it's his money you are borrowing!

GETTING TO KNOW YOU

If you seek a bank loan, the banker will ask you some pointy questions. If you have borrowed money before, did you pay it back? On time? Have you ever gone through bankruptcy? Health, serious family problems? Have you any experiences in the field of your proposed business? Your answers to such questions matter and will affect your chances for a loan. Except for small, signature loans, your past record, reputation, and experiences will be considered when you apply for a larger loan.

MAKE IT EASY

One reason you should carefully prepare your information about your business is that some banks are not too crazy about making small business loans in the first place, because of the small return they get for their work. A small loan may take as much of their time as a large one, which would make them more profit. Lots of little loans can be a nuisance.

Have some consideration for your lender. Be sure you have a short, simple, clear business plan in writing which you can hand him when you go to see him. Be sure the plan describes your financial needs and your expected income, not just what you plan to make or do. Put yourself in his shoes: would *you* loan *you* the money, based on what you say about your plan?

MANY BANKERS ARE HUMAN

Don't write off your local banker until he has said no, plainly. Bankers vary greatly. Some are very community-conscious. They want to see their town or area grow and not just because they hope to make more money. They feel an obligation to help. They may even be interested in the particular kind of business you hope to start. Many of them understand that sometimes small start-up businesses grow into very large ones, who will remember who helped them get started.

PUBLIC LENDERS

Almost every state and many counties and towns have an office set up to encourage the development of small businesses. There are offices or persons in state and local governmental agencies whose job it is to try to help new businesses get started in order to create jobs and build the local tax base, increase retail sales and whatnot. Ask around, at the town hall and courthouse.

COMMUNITY DEVELOPMENT ORGANIZATIONS

In South Dakota there are over 140 local economic development organizations. Nearly every county seat has one; some are publicly supported, most are not. Some are county-wide, some include several counties. There is a directory of these groups; ask at your library. All of them are eager to see new businesses in their areas. Unfortunately for many of them, they think mainly in terms of moving established, going businesses to their town or area, rather than taking a serious look at the possibilities for tiny, one-person and family business start-ups that are possible right under their noses. Many have a fairly narrowly defined definition in their minds as to what constitutes a "business." They see very tiny businesses as unimportant, which will not create much of a stir, in their minds. And they tend to favor the kinds of traditional businesses which they understand. As one can imagine, the interests of these groups vary with the people who make them up. One just about has to go check them out before knowing whether or not they care about being of any help. Ask the local mayor or commissioner who they are and where to find them.

PUBLIC HELP AGENCIES

There are a number of public agencies that can be of help. The federal Small Business Administration, located in Sioux Falls, has a long history of helping small business with management questions. They publish a great many informational pamphlets and books, full of information to help start-up businesses. While the SBA has no minimum amount for the size of loans, it approves, in practice, very few loans for less than $5,000.00.

Other public agencies that may have loan funds include the State Department of Agriculture and the Governor's Office for Economic Development, both located in Pierre. The Rural Development Office of the Federal Department of Agriculture (formerly called the Farmers Home Administration), Huron, may have funds for some purposes. And be sure to check out the offices of the six Planning and Development Districts. They have offices in Aberdeen, Sisseton, Yankton, Sioux Falls, Watertown, and Rapid City. A major feature of their work is encouraging new small businesses. Some federal departments like Transportation make loans and grants for special purposes. Native Tribal governments may have funds available for enrolled tribal members, from their own funds, or from federal agencies.

BANKS SUPPLY THE ACTUAL MONEY

Most public agencies, state and federal, are simply guarantors for the loans they approve; they provide no actual cash. The actual cash comes from a bank. One has to go to a local bank and get approval for the loan first. If the loan is granted, the public agency may also approve it. If they do, they simply serve to guarantee repayment of your loan to the bank. In effect, they are co-signers of the note, to insure the loan for the lender. But you have to find—and get past—the bank making the loan, before anything else happens. Some private, non-profit development groups have their own loan funds, but the applicant screening process isn't greatly different.

LONG SHOTS

In seeking loan funds, it doesn't hurt to inquire of local non-profit and advocacy agencies, which are organized to assist women, minorities, seniors, and ethnic and special interest groups. These would include farm organizations, church and fraternal groups, and the like. One never knows. Something might turn up.

PRIVATE FOUNDATIONS

Some people, having heard about large grants made by private, non-profit foundations, wonder if it might be possible to "get a grant" to help start their new business. In general, forget it. Such grants by foundations are virtually unknown. Foundations may give funds to study health problems, ways to improve the economy in a given area, to stop soil erosion, improve services to youth or a thousand other things, but they do not give funds to private individuals to start up their own profit-making businesses. If they did, the lines of applicants would stretch from here to Mars.

RELATIVES AND FRIENDS

Those people closest to us are often the first stop in seeking start-up funds for a small business. If you have family, relatives, or friends who can afford to loan money, this can help. They are often willing to accept a lower rate of interest and a better time schedule for repayment than you could get from a commercial lender. And they may be able to help you to set up or operate the business, if they have an interest in it.

Borrowing from relatives and friends may not be all roses. If things don't work out, it can lead to bad feelings that can last a long time. And you may get more advice in running the business than you would like. Few things can make an expert as quickly as making an investment in a project.

The one certain thing you must do if you borrow from a relative or friend: be sure you have an agreement on paper. Be sure they understand what you plan to do. Do not allow yourself to accept funds unless the terms are clear and written: how much, at what interest, and for how long. Unless you do this, you are almost certain to have problems later.

VENTURE CAPITAL LENDERS

Generally, you can forget anything you may have heard about this source of start-up capital. The true venture capital lender is not interested in new start-up businesses. Such lenders look for not-so-small businesses that already have a very successful financial track record of several years standing, with high profits, in a rapid growth field. They usually expect to sell their interest in the business at a high profit, in a short, specified number of years. Besides, there are very few such lenders in South Dakota. Don't look for hope there.

SEED MONEY LENDERS

Seed money is usually high risk money, because it is used to start up a business without any certainty that it will succeed. People who supply seed money may be interested in the type of business you propose. Very often, they are friends or relatives. They may have an entrepreneurial bent themselves and they probably have imagination. Such lenders understand that the risks are very real, but they are willing to gamble on the prospects. Hopefully, they should be able to withstand the loss if things don't pay out.

IN GENERAL, ON MONEY

Don't borrow more or less than you need. If you don't have to, don't borrow at all. When you borrow, you have to pay it back, with interest and, somehow, you have to earn the funds to do that. Don't borrow too early, before you actually need the money. Borrowing isn't evil; it is often wise and necessary. Always have a plan as to how you will handle the payments that isn't based entirely on hope.

Prompt and timely repayment of your loans will establish a good credit rating for you and will enable you to borrow increasingly larger amounts should you need them. You will be able to establish lines of credit with your lender, which can help smooth out the rough spots in your financial year. The more reliable and dependable you are in repaying loans and in paying your bills in general, the more willing lenders and suppliers will become in helping you along. So, respect the agreements you make and give these people reason to have confidence and respect for you.

ALL THINGS COME...

Today, life moves much faster than in our parents' time. It's getting harder to find people who will accept the proverb that "all things come to those who wait." Americans are becoming increasingly impatient. We want quick answers and faster cures. We want to lose 35 pounds in ten days. No matter that Grandpa worked all his life to pay for the farm. We want fast success.

Some small business start-ups fail because the starters lack the patience to hang in and make it happen. They misjudge the time it takes for the public—buyers—to realize they exist, to size them up and decide to give them a try. They expect to take profits too soon and are not willing to do without during the first tough months.

One can, of course, try for too long a time. But, usually, if one listens to customers, suppliers, and others who come and go at the business, it's possible to get a sense of whether your plan will work or not. If you have done a good job of testing your product before launch, you will have learned much to guide you on how to proceed. Remember, Ben Franklin once said, "He that can have patience can have what he will."

EPILOGUE

In a world in which most human organizations seem driven, lemming-like, to become larger—to merge and merge again—to increase their "share" of influence, sales, net profits, and power within their industry, the tone and the suggestions in this book will seem counter. It proposes that you buck the trend, step out of the crowd, resist the flow, and swim upstream.

Going on your own isn't for everyone. Some folks just don't feel assured enough that their instincts and judgement are right. After all, if nearly everyone is doing it, must that not be the right way to go?

Let us be plain: running a tiny business in a tiny community in rural South Dakota is not the direction to go if you want a life of glamour, intensity, fast action, high visibility, bright lights, social and political power, or glitzy consumption. If these are what you want, better make a U-turn now.

Be certain that even if you want a life in a rural, quiet, serene simple setting, close to nature and far from relentless urban rush, running your own business in such a setting is not an endless delight. So, check all the dials and see if they read right. Would you really like to run your own show?

If it's still green and go:

1. Decide when you have done enough planning and when it's time to *do.*

2. Go back to the chapters on model building and testing. Be sure you have a model or a plan of organization that reflects what you want to do. You must be able to show it to others.

3. Get going on market testing. Even if your product works, try to learn if anyone will buy it. You must know this.

4. If people show that they will buy and that they want the product you offer, start producing and learn to market it.

5. When you have done these things, you will find that you won't have to decide when to start: you will already be underway!

GOOD LUCK AND GODSPEED!

ACKNOWLEDGEMENTS

One often hears experienced teachers say that they have learned more from their students than they were able to give back. There have been many professionals and experts in agriculture, economic development, finance, and rural life who have given much to shape the ideas in this book. Most of all, there are many hundreds of people all over rural South Dakota who have helped write it. These people are on the ground, starting and running small businesses in nearly every county, helping to build our new rural communities. They are immensely practical, resourceful people, who focus on what is sensible and possible—now. They are kind, open, friendly, hopeful people—the best possible exhibit of a way of life they are working hard to maintain and preserve.

This publication has been greatly assisted through the generosity of the Land O'Lakes Foundation, which provided important encouragement and financial assistance toward its production.

I want to express appreciation to the directors of the Association of Christian Churches of South Dakota for their patient support of the Rural Initiative Center over the years during which this book was being formed.

Especially, I would like to thank my wife, Lorna, who has endured much to support my years of criss-crossing the vast reaches of rural South Dakota.

THE RURAL INITIATIVE CENTER

South Dakota is the nation's most agriculturally dependent state. Changes in the technology of farm production and in world agricultural markets have placed severe pressure on farm people. Many have been forced to leave the land. Decreasing rural population threatens many community services including schools, health and government services. Rural families must develop new ways of producing income—new businesses and services.

Most rural families live in South Dakota by choice. They would like to continue to do so, rather than be forced to move to a city to find work. The Rural Initiative Center was established to help rural families develop new sources of income to enable them to stay in their communities.

The Rural Initiative Center is a private, non-profit agency which seeks to increase farm, ranch and small town family income in South Dakota. The Center provides information, technical assistance and consultative services to rural people to help them to create new or expand existing small businesses. The Center encourages diversity in new ideas and methods of all types of small business, including specialized agricultural production, processing and marketing, which will result in value-added products or needed services.

The Rural Initiative Center is an integral service of the Association of Christian Churches of South Dakota, which is supported by ten major church denominations whose combined memberships include a majority of the state's population.

Any individual or family who seeks to start or expand a small business on a farm, ranch, or in a small town in South Dakota, to increase personal or family income, is eligible for help. There are no unwritten or implied obligations which are conditions for assistance.